Imaginati
Admired cities, s

Robert Govers

Imaginative Communities:
Admired cities, regions and countries

ISBN: 978-90-828265-2-4 (pbk)
ISBN: 978-90-828265-0-0 (hbk)
ISBN: 978-90-828265-1-7 (ebk)

Keywords:
1. Governance; 2. Community reputation; 3. Mental geography; 4. Media;
5. International relations; 6. Globalisation; 7. Popular beliefs and psychology

DEWEY / BISAC Codes:
900 / SOC015000 Social Science: Human Geography
070 / BUS070060 Business & Economics: Industries – Media & Communications
327 / POL011000 Political Science: International Relations – General

Published by
Reputo Press
Antwerp, Belgium

Cover image inspired by Latifa Echakhch's art installation
Empty Flags

Edited by Povey Editorial, Devon, United Kingdom

In memory of Frank M. Go (1948–2017)

With special thanks to Simon Anholt, Martin Boisen, Erik van 't Klooster, Axel Van Noten, and Keith Povey for their input and critical reflections.

Contents

Chapter 1
How we appreciate here and there

Communities with imagination are beacons of hope in a ruthless, competitive and globalised world in which identities seem lost.

Today people are uprooted and they question the meaning of community. Is the USA still the land of freedom and opportunity? Is Paris still the city of romance? The United Kingdom a global power of significance? The Netherlands the model country for a progressive tolerant world, with Amsterdam as the capital of open-mindedness? Syria and Iraq's Mesopotamia the cradle of civilisation? Rio de Janeiro the party capital of the world? The Himalayas the centre of spirituality?

At the same time, some communities are emerging from the shadows, challenging stereotypes. Dubai as a global hub of post-modernity, contradicting Arab stereotypes. The shimmering capital of Kazakhstan, Astana, and its successful bicycle racing team, versus cliché images of nomads on horses and yurts. Laptop and *Lederhosen* in German Bavaria. The Smart City of Medellín, Colombia, versus images of drug cartels and violence. Disorganised India as the world's computer helpdesk.

Yet, clichéd and stereotypical images of internationally well-known communities are being exploited for commercial gain by resort, entertainment and real estate developers, but also online. Think of the Venetian resorts in Vegas and Macau; Holland Village as one of the nine towns projects in Shanghai; the Chinese replica of Austria's Alpine village of Hallstatt in Guangdong province; or driving through Los Angeles in Grand Theft Auto V. In all the noise in (social) media, exploiting well-known mental associations and consumer trust among global audiences is an easy way to get attention and build reputation. In management terms one might say that some communities face an exploitation of their "brand equity" and an infringement of their "trademark", if it was not for the fact that these "brands" usually remain legally unprotected.

So, increasingly, our understanding of the world is challenged and blurred. A lot of this confusion is, of course, caused by globalisation.

11

1.1 Why we got lost

Globalisation is caused by increased international flows of money, people, technology and media. The global financial meltdown after 2008 clearly revealed how connected the global financial system is and that money goes where investments generate most profit against acceptable risks. When the subprime mortgage crisis hit the United States in 2008, money flowed into the city of Dubai, where land sales peaked to US$16 billion, only to drop to US$6 billion in 2009[1] when it became clear that the resource-rich Arabian Gulf region was not immune to the global financial meltdown. Also, to get an idea of how globalised the financial system has become and where the money went, just look at which countries FIFA has selected as hosts for the football World Cup since 2006 (Germany): South Africa, Brazil, Russia, Qatar. Not exactly the usual suspects, but countries with uncommitted resources at the time.

Meanwhile we have become accustomed to extensive global media coverage with satellite channels such as CNN, NBC, BBC World, but also China Global Television Network (formerly CCTV Int.), RT (formerly Russia Today) or Al Jazeera. It has resulted in people everywhere increasingly seeing themselves as global citizens (see Table 1), massively boosting migration. According to the United Nations, the number of persons living in a country other than where they were born reached 244 million in 2015 for the world as a whole, a 41 per cent increase compared to 2000. Twenty million of the 244 million migrants are refugees. Lastly, globalisation can also be observed in the use of technology. In 2000 two-thirds of the online world population was from Europe or North America. In 2010 two-thirds of the online world population was from elsewhere.

This leads to the conclusion that cities, regions and countries no longer compete based on functional characteristics such as accessibility, service levels, access to finance, technological advancement, cost benefits or knowledge. The following examples clearly illustrate this. The International Air Transport Association has claimed that the Arabian Gulf region has become the worldwide hub for airline and airport innovation with rapid growth, major new infrastructural investment, and carriers such as Qatar Airways, Emirates Airline and Etihad Airways rapidly expanding their networks. These are the players that are setting new service standards, in the same way as Asian hotel brands are moving to Europe and North America. When it comes to material goods, delocalisation of manufacturing and assembly plants towards Asia or Latin America is no longer just a matter of aiming for lower cost, but also of being where the market is, as Western economies continue to slump. And it is not just a matter of low-wage, blue-collar work. In India, each year around eight million students complete higher education. In China this number is twelve million, with Brazil in third place with "only" one million graduates coming out of tertiary education.[2]

Table 1: Global citizenship and tolerance according to World Values Survey (conducted in 50 countries)[3]

	Yes
I see myself as a world citizen	74.1%
Important child qualities: Tolerance and respect for other people	68.8%
Would not mind to have as neighbours: People from a different race	81.5%
Would not mind to have as neighbours: People from a different religion	77.5%
Would not mind to have as neighbours: Immigrants/foreign workers	76.0%
Would not mind to have as neighbours: People who speak a different language	83.2%

Hence, the world is increasingly interconnected and globalisation has led to homogenisation, which raises the question: what is the relevance of communities and geographies? Because of globalisation our day-to-day work, private life, political participation or cultural identity have also been uprooted as local functions onto the global stage. Political participation in many countries in 2016 and 2017 (examples include Brexit, Trump, Erdoğan) has shown that globalisation has led to feelings of insecurity and a sense of loss of solidarity. But it has also confirmed that many of us are still looking for a sense of belonging (identity), authenticity, and stability and safety. Building a community and its reputation – to be held in high esteem internationally – might therefore be more relevant than ever.

1.2 How we can regain control

In a world characterised by homogenisation, Disneyfication and McDonaldization, the counter-movement is to advance the international success of uniquely local creations. Think of the Slow Movement and Cittaslow. There are numerous examples of cultural and culinary produce with local character, which, by definition, appeal to an acquired taste and are relatively costly but are nevertheless internationally renowned and in demand. These elements of identity can also become dominant clichés as part of international stereotypes. French wine and cheese, Mongolian cashmere, British heritage, Chinese fireworks, Belgian chocolate and beer, Dutch tulips and Masters, Colombian coffee, Russian literature, Egyptian pyramids, Swiss watches; the list is endless. Cultural productions that are linked to local identities have also become big business and a source of local pride. Neo-liberal supranational entities such as the European Union have even created the systems that allow communities to protect their traditional produce from the competition (such as in the case of champagne, Rioja wine or feta cheese).

So while globalisation has caused us to feel uprooted, community identity and civic pride seem to provide some stability, as unquestionable *raisons d'être*. But are they? In his seminal work *Imagined Communities*, published in 1983, Benedict Anderson argues that even identity and civic pride are imagined and manipulated. Anderson's analysis specifically deals with nationalism as being socially constructed within a community (through the printed narrative of the nation, shared language, museums and education systems). The nation is something that is imagined as a comradeship by the people who perceive themselves as part of it, even when they do not know most of the other members. It is argued that as religions and empires lost their grip on society, civic leaders needed to construct identities for people to rally behind. When building the nation state, this encouraged nationalism, but the same can be argued for civic pride generally. The question is: what will sustain community self-respect when governments lose authority in a globalising world?

People want to be part of a community that they can be proud of and – in a world with global and social media – that pride is increasingly influenced by how communities are being talked about outside, as opposed to how they are imagined within. In today's interconnected world, communities that gain respect are those that contribute to humanity and the planet at large (examples of which are provided in Chapter 2). Will virtue, as opposed to nationalism, religion or power, therefore become the driving force behind local identity construction and global image projection?

It seems to be counter-intuitive, because in the neo-liberal management-driven world that we live in, everything has to be measured in economic terms, and policy makers and public institutions made accountable, reflecting the principles and ideals of the private sector. While being pushed to be lean and agile, we are supposed to measure our achievements against goals and those goals have to be SMART (specific, measurable, achievable, relevant, time-bound). But the question is: how do we deal with soft targets? What if we aim for goals that are not so specific and easy to measure, such as happiness, virtue, civic pride or perception? Too often such objectives are swept aside as too vague, too soppy and too difficult. For many, this is common sense. However, to use a Frank Underwood (*House of Cards*) quote, 'There is only one problem with common sense, it is so... common'. The consequence is that we end up with standardised policies, proven solutions, copy-paste behaviour and a rat race for the latest, tallest and "smartest" icon that will generate fifteen minutes of fame. Community governance, leadership and engagement generally, have just become so boring in the last few decades. We need to reinvigorate the role of and importance assigned to imagination; to imagine what communities with a strong sense of belonging can accomplish internationally.

To use another Underwood quote, 'Imagination is its own form of courage'. Imaginative communities have the courage to be bold, the creativity to come up with new ideas, the power to innovate and be different, without disavowing local character, but by exploiting and reinforcing it. This requires leadership, in government, but equally in the private sector and civil society – and hence collaboration. It requires leadership that understands that local interests are best served by aligning them with each other and with global developments, through collaboration. That is the way in which actions lead to improved reputation, admiration and pride in the long term, besides performance improvement or economic gain in the short term.

The idea of imaginative communities therefore aims to advance the idea of the *Imagined Communities* that Anderson wrote about. It is about making the local relevant globally as well as locally. It is possible to do that, because at the end of the day all is imagined anyway. The Sceptic philosophers have known that for centuries. This idea of bridging the gap between reality and perception and how it can be influenced by experience and communication is not new at all: it has long been a major topic of discussion among philosophers. Descartes, as the founder of modern philosophy, could be regarded as the progenitor of the ideas presented in this book, as he lays the foundation for representative realism which contends that our ideas are valid or relevant only when they correspond to the reality of the world around us. Sceptics like Locke, Hume, Bayle or Berkeley, however, argue that there is no proof of the existence of an outside material world: we only have perceptual knowledge through our senses. Hence they agree with Descartes when he claims that 'to be is to be perceived'. Similarly, idealists such as Kant believe that physical things exist only in the sense that they are perceived. This leads to constructivism, in which knowledge and image are personal constructs and hence perceptions and – as a result – realities are subjective. This is further emphasised by existentialists such as Kierkegaard, Husserl, Brentano or Heidegger, who believe that all that matters is that humans actively participate in the world; "being there" or *Dasein*. This pursuit of "presence" is what this book is about.

1.3 What imaginative communities?

Imaginative communities are neighbourhoods, cities, regions and countries – possibly even continents – that reinforce or build local character and civic pride, while at the same time captivating outsiders (external publics). "Community" is defined by the *Random House Unabridged Dictionary* as 'a social group of any size whose members reside in a specific locality, share government, and often have a common cultural and historical heritage'; and 'the locality inhabited by such a group'. In simple terms, I use the concept of "community" to refer to a people that feel that they belong together, linked to a locality (including diaspora) and (often) shared government. Hence, "community" potentially refers to nation, country and state at the same time respectively or simultaneously. Yet, neighbourhoods, towns, cities and regions are also "communities" in the context of this book.

"Imaginative" refers to members and stakeholders of such a community using their imagination in order to envisage and accomplish creative, unconventional, original, inventive and – most importantly – uniquely local initiatives, projects, events, infrastructures or policies that reinforce the *community* and the way it is perceived by outsiders. Imaginative communities that produce a constant stream of such innate initiatives acquire a unique positioning in the minds of global audiences, as they affirm distinctive mental associations. These associations can be linked uniquely to the geography, the people or their government (i.e. country, nation, state or other scalar levels) separately or simultaneously, depending on local circumstances.

Examples of imaginative community initiatives covered in this book are:

- Estonia adapting its constitution to include internet access as a human right and allowing e-residency, to emphasise the country's tech-savvy nature compared to other countries in the Baltic region.
- Bhutan, a country where wellbeing has long been prioritised over material gain, inventing and institutionalising the idea of gross national happiness.
- Dubai's man-made islands in the shape of palm trees, which traditionally represent the source of life in the region around the Arabian Gulf.
- The Hague, international city of peace and justice, creating the peace festival and cyber-security delta.
- Austin's South by Southwest (SXSW) Festival as a celebration of the city's musical roots.
- Migrants and refugees building their genuine "land of the free": the United States of America.
- The Dutch city of Den Bosch mobilising everything and everyone in 2016 to commemorate the death of Hieronymus Bosch, one of the most influential Dutch Masters of all time, who died in 1516 in the city that gave him his name.
- The pyramids and the Forum as representations of Egyptian and Roman cultural identity, religion and scientific achievements of their time.
- Oslo's *Future Library*, where a thousand trees have been planted just outside the city to supply paper for a special anthology of books to be printed in one hundred years' time. In the meantime, each year one author contributes a

manuscript, which is held in a trust, unpublished, until 2114, to reflect the city's forward-looking mentality and mantra that the best is yet to come.

- Finland creating its own set of emoticons to express emotional aspects of Finnishness on social media and on mobile devices anywhere in the world, reflecting the tech-savvy and quirky, fun-loving nature of the Finns.
- The House of Medici building the home of the Renaissance in Florence, with the Duomo di Firenze (Cattedrale di Santa Maria del Fiore) as one of the first examples of captivating iconic masterpiece structures built to attract visitors to the city state.
- Gaudí's Barcelona or Manrique's Lanzarote.
- The Dutch province of Limburg – a region that, over the course of its history, has learned to live with nearby and shifting international borders – organising cross-border design, arts and sports projects.
- The Van Gogh-inspired "starry night" cycle path in Eindhoven, the city of lights in the Netherlands. The path is paved with fluorescent stones that light up at night to resemble the painting by Van Gogh, who lived in the area.

What imaginative communities need is:
- a sense of identity, belonging and virtue
- by which to influence international perceptions
- with access to mainstream and social media buzz
- by building unique experiences
- through imagination and leadership
- and community collaboration.

All these cases and requirements are covered in detail in this book.

Reading guide

The essence of what imaginative communities are about is covered in chapters 2 to 4 where most examples are also presented. Chapter 2 is essentially about communities and chapter 3 about imagination. Both come together in chapter 4, imaginative communities.

Chapters 5 to 8 dig deeper and provide background and conceptual underpinning. They elaborate on how communities build image/reputation/perceptions (chapter 5), how communities project image/communicate/set the media agenda (chapter 6), how communities are experienced (chapter 7) and how communities are enlightened (chapter 8).

Chapter 2
Who we are: Imagined communities

Admiration is attained by those communities that have a strong sense of belonging, virtue and achievement.

What most admired communities have in common is that they foster a strong sense of identity, belonging and comradeship among their members. This seems to be a prerequisite for communities' ability to build a strong reputation internationally. Identity might be imagined – i.e. politically influenced – to some extent, but it is also likely to be grounded in some shared geography, history and mentality of the people. As a result, it facilitates a shared sense of direction and local culture, often linked to moral virtue and universal human goals. I will argue in this chapter that communities that are subsequently successful in achieving those goals through continuous consistent action get noticed internationally, particularly if their achievements are in some way imaginative, remarkable or extraordinary.

2.1 Our pride

Community pride is referred to as *campanilismo* in Italian. Nationalism is the *campanilismo* of the nation. The *campanile* is the bell tower that dominates the skyline of many towns and cities in Italy. *Campanilismo* is the attachment that people feel to that locality: a sense of pride and appreciation of tradition. Unfortunately, it can also be interpreted and deliberately instrumentalised in negative ways: as in parochialism or rivalry towards neighbours and the need to defend local values that are threatened by "others". However, while parochialism is the direct translation of *campanilismo* in English, the Italian word does not have the negative connotation of parochialism as narrow-mindedness, provincialism or being unsophisticated. Nationalism, obviously, is tainted excessively with negative associations such as xenophobia or bigotry, which is unfortunate, because a sense of belonging, identity and comradeship is not necessarily a bad thing. The danger lies in the fact that it can be manipulated and fired up.

This is what Anderson argues in his book *Imagined Communities*. The city, region or nation as community is imagined, because the members of most communities (apart from the smallest rural villages) do not all really know each other, yet there is the idea of communion and connectedness. Nationalism specifically filled the void left after the retreat of religion or the dynastic realms as default frames of reference in the nineteenth century. For people to imagine a sense of community became important as an organising principle; it was constructed through the use of flags, language, museums, anthems, traditions, education systems and the rest of it.

In the age of globalisation, homogenisation and delocalisation, community pride and the link to identity are reappearing on the public agenda. It is remarkable though that while calls for a reinvigoration of national identities are seen as controversial, this is not the case with local identities and *campanilismo*. Community identity linked to cities and regions might just prove to be more promising than national identities. Might it be a fruitful compromise between glorifying the nation state and the cosmopolitan commercialisation of cities?[4] In any case, community attachment can be formed at many levels and, depending on whom and where people are, the city, the region, the country, the continent or the village might take priority. Living in Belgium, I am constantly reminded by my neighbours, friends and family that I am a Dutchman (the Dutch are generally not very popular among the Flemish). However, having lived abroad in Africa, Asia and Europe and being married to a Belgian wife for over twenty years I hardly feel Dutch anymore, myself. I like to think and say that I am a global citizen, but having had the privilege of travelling to many countries, I came to realise that my frame of reference is actually very continental. I am possibly most attached to being European and to the cosmopolitan city of Antwerp where I live now. In other words, attachments are both personal and socially and culturally determined.

Table 2 expands on this. People in many communities seem to be perfectly able to feel attached to the nation, the local or a multinational community all at the same time. The Jordanians, for instance, are generally individualistic, yet they feel attached to and proud of their nation and their local community, and they feel part of the Arab Union, all at the same time. The majority of Russians are far less attached to the local or individualism, but are more nationalistic. Uzbeks and Moroccans are not at all individualistic, but much attached to their vicinity and the nation; and even though the Swedes are highly individualistic, they also feel part of their local community, the nation, as well as the European Union. Yet, these are generalisations and individuals will have their own sentiments.

Table 2: Multiple levels of community attachment according to the World Values Survey[3]

Country	I am proud of my nationality	I see myself as part of my local community	I see myself as part of my nation	I see myself as an autonomous individual	I see myself as part of a regional international union of nations
Algeria	95.9%	81.5%	94.6%	70.3%	78.6%
Armenia	96.9%	97.4%	98.1%	86.9%	58.7%
Australia	96.0%	88.1%	96.8%	69.0%	62.7%
Azerbaijan	92.3%	39.6%	95.2%	64.8%	20.4%
Belarus	81.8%	21.0%	89.8%	29.3%	51.0%
Chile	93.7%	90.4%	94.8%	78.1%	37.4%
China	89.6%	95.2%	97.6%	91.7%	80.7%
Colombia	97.0%	90.8%	97.5%	81.9%	
Cyprus (T)	91.0%	93.6%	95.6%	82.9%	76.4%
Ecuador	98.4%	93.3%	96.3%	88.6%	91.9%
Egypt	96.5%	94.5%	98.2%	66.0%	59.0%
Estonia	73.3%	78.5%	98.9%	61.7%	84.7%
Germany	79.0%	79.0%	87.0%	83.0%	57.0%
Ghana	99.2%	99.2%	99.7%	65.5%	93.8%
Iraq	90.6%	93.6%	89.0%	64.5%	63.3%
Japan	71.6%	97.9%	98.8%	89.2%	
Jordan	98.9%	96.7%	95.9%	86.2%	91.9%
Kazakhstan	94.8%	36.3%	96.5%	34.1%	48.6%
Kuwait	97.0%	90.1%	92.2%	77.7%	
Kyrgyzstan	96.0%	81.9%	93.9%	74.0%	67.8%
Lebanon	80.9%	73.6%	81.6%	73.5%	53.5%
Libya	94.9%	96.3%	98.3%	82.1%	
Malaysia	96.8%	98.1%	96.6%	91.5%	70.8%
Mexico	95.3%	92.5%	95.9%	71.9%	62.4%
Morocco	92.1%	94.6%	99.0%	14.0%	63.5%
Netherlands	83.7%	78.9%	93.6%	83.5%	59.4%
Nigeria	93.3%	96.8%	97.4%	79.1%	88.4%
Pakistan	95.9%	87.5%	92.6%	79.3%	78.3%
Palestine	96.9%	89.9%	92.6%	74.0%	78.1%
Peru	93.3%	90.8%	98.0%	82.0%	

Country	I am proud of my nationality	I see myself as part of my local community	I see myself as part of my nation	I see myself as an autonomou s individual	I see myself as part of a regional internation al union of nations
Philippines	98.0%	93.0%	97.1%	90.7%	70.4%
Poland	95.9%	94.3%	97.8%	84.1%	85.0%
Qatar	100.0%	99.2%	100.0%	94.2%	98.9%
Romania	83.6%	83.5%	86.8%	68.9%	66.0%
Russia	80.5%	27.2%	93.8%	27.7%	44.0%
Rwanda	99.3%	88.9%	89.7%	69.7%	79.4%
Singapore	89.4%	87.6%	93.4%	70.6%	69.9%
Slovenia	89.3%	92.6%	96.2%	88.9%	82.6%
South Korea	90.9%	87.3%	93.3%	63.4%	
Spain	91.8%	97.0%	94.8%	87.2%	93.5%
Sweden	87.7%	92.4%	97.5%	92.3%	77.8%
Taiwan	71.0%	94.7%	98.1%	91.2%	91.6%
Tunisia	94.2%	91.2%	95.9%	83.6%	87.9%
Turkey	97.3%	92.0%	90.1%	69.0%	40.3%
Ukraine	71.3%	52.4%	86.4%	37.3%	52.0%
United States	91.4%	87.1%	95.6%	67.6%	83.8%
Uruguay	93.5%	87.4%	96.7%	69.0%	58.1%
Uzbekistan	99.4%	90.6%	99.1%	4.2%	67.6%
Yemen	96.1%	96.5%	96.4%	67.4%	95.6%
Zimbabwe	96.0%	93.6%	98.0%	51.3%	80.9%

In some countries all this is even more complex though. As Table 3 illustrates, in Belgium, the Flemish (citizens of the northern Dutch-speaking region of Flanders) are significantly more attached to their Flemish region than the Belgian French-speaking community is attached to Wallonia (in the south of the country). Partly as a result of that, on average, the Walloons seem to be prouder of king and country than the Flemish are. The people of Brussels have their own stories, being a mix of Flemish, Walloons and migrants from everywhere. Hence, community pride, even though it is strengthened by collective emotions, is a private and complex phenomenon that can consist of multiple levels of attachment.

Table 3: Belgian respondents' geographical attachment (percentage of respondents indicating attachment with first and second choice combined)[5]

Respondents' origin and age	Flanders		Wallonia		Brussels	
	18–30 y.	+60y.	18–30 y.	+60 y.	18–30 y.	+60 y.
Municipality	58	60	49	56	28	35
Region	62	61	28	42	47	49
Belgium	49	49	58	67	54	62
Europe	15	12	33	20	29	36
The world	9	6	24	8	26	11

So why has nationalism received such a bad rap, if we are perfectly okay with people cheering for their city, their region or themselves? In and of itself it does not seem to be harmful to build community pride; but it can become problematic if abused by authoritarians and populists (see Altemeyer's 2006 book *The Authoritarians*). The pride in one's nation, which, in itself, is largely invented and nurtured anyway, combined with hubris, can easily be abused to include sentiments of superiority, ethnocentricity, and the application of othering (us versus them). It is a risky cocktail, easily exploited at the hands of authoritarian leaders or populists, as history has repeatedly shown to this day. Presumably, such exploitation is generally the domain of the nation state because of access to absolute power, the military and the treasury. Community pride at sub-national levels seems to be less at risk, although there are exceptions of course, considering, for instance, Flemish nationalism or the American south (see page 54). Also, if we add the increasing importance of cities and regions into this mix (with access to treasury, welfare provision, etc.) this might not hold true in the long run.

Regardless of such risks, community building can be a good idea in order for people to share purpose, partnership and prosperity. However, in today's world it would make absolute sense and show moral leadership if communities incorporated diversity, openness and open-mindedness into their *raison d'être*. It is risky when it is exclusive, ethnocentric or based on dogmatic religious beliefs which facilitate double standards and compartmentalisation into in- and out-groups. Inclusive and approachable is the way to go in a globalised world.

2.2 Our shared identity

National, regional or local identity is an elusive and controversial topic. It is hard to define and is often seen as being similar in meaning to concepts such as community spirit, local uniqueness, distinctiveness, local character, *couleur locale*, *genius loci* or sense of belonging. Also, identity is obviously not static, but is versatile and contested. Rather than attempting an all-encompassing one-liner definition, it seems more useful to elaborate on where community identity can be found. Based on earlier studies, a categorisation of identity elements is listed in Table 4. It is a collage that can be used to find underlying narratives.

Table 4: Constructive elements of community identity[6]

Structural (static)	Semi-static (change slowly over time)	Changing signifiers (change easily, but reflect deeper meaning)	Colouring (fluid elements)
Location	Size	Great events/ Great heroes	Past symbolism
History	Physical appearance	Food / Architecture / Arts /	Past behaviour
	Inner mentality	Literature / Popular culture	Communication
		Language / Traditions /	
		Rituals / Folk	

It is my firm belief that every community has its own uniqueness and the potential to use its identity in imaginative ways. The way that the above model can assist in surfacing such distinctiveness is illustrated in the following cases.

Cross-border Limburg

In a project in the Dutch province of Limburg in which I was involved (together with Simon Anholt and Jeremy Hildreth), the above approach quickly led to consensus about the uniqueness of the region. Limburg, The Netherlands is a province that functions as a Dutch cross-border corridor into the heart of Europe. Today, the region of Limburg interfaces with Belgium and Germany as well as Luxembourg and France, but it has dealt with shifting borders constantly over the course of its history. Limburg has had a major impact on European borders in the past, yet residents feel a strong sense of connectedness. The annual Provincial Census asks respondents to what extent they feel connected with the province and surrounding regions. This is reflected in Table 5. The results, which change very little year on year, show that Limburgers are very much attached to their province, much more so than Dutch citizens in other provinces.

Table 5: The Limburgers and their province, compared to residents in other provinces in the Netherlands. Source: Provincie Limburg (2012) Census.

	Positive responses in Limburg	Positive responses in other Dutch provinces
I feel connected with my community/province	87%	81%
I am a proud member of my community/province	92%	79%
I feel connected with Germany and/or Belgium	79%	

According to another *Provincial Monitor*,[7] 95% of the population feels at home in the province and people are primarily attached to their municipality ($^1/_3$), province ($^1/_3$) or the Netherlands/Europe/world ($^1/_3$). At the same time, a two-fold emancipation from the Catholic Church and the state has been experienced, resulting in a sense of abandonment. It signals the paradox between strong local identity versus interregional and international dependency and cooperation.

Borders are part of the regional identity and provide Limburg with opportunities for a unique positioning. It is striking that many properties that the Dutch label as "typically Limburg" (carnival, religion, culture, dialect, hills) are shared with the surrounding German and Belgian regions. Yet, contact and kinship with the neighbours has waned over time. The number of young Limburgers who still speak the German language has significantly decreased over time and is currently perceived as a roadblock for Euregional cooperation.

Such paradoxical discussions about borders and local identity also took place in the focus group discussion with experts on the region's local identity. In Limburg, international borders have constantly shifted over the years as a result of several different forces, not least political forces. This has resulted in local populations looking for a sense of place and a place of their own. In that respect, Limburgers could be described as local cosmopolitans. They are used to an environment in which international loyalties change, while, at the same time, for stability, people focus on their own church and their own local community and little else outside. Hence, paradoxically, while residents and entrepreneurs feel the Euregional bond with neighbours, the creation of the Dutch nation state increased the sense of regional identity restricted by borders, also administratively.

In 1831, Sebastiaan Van Beringen[8] wrote: 'the 4th of June, the prince of Saksen-Coburg has been elected king of Belgians and has made his arrival, under the name of Leopold I, in Brussels on July 21st. This is the fourth sovereign house that I have experienced to rule Roermond, since 40 years. We were first imperial (Austrian), then we became French, then to become Dutch again, and now we are Belgian.'

Only eight years later Van Beringen would experience his fifth change in nationality, when what is currently Dutch Limburg would finally become part of the Kingdom of the Netherlands as it is today, although it also remained part of the German Bund for a while. Even as late as 1906 the province was still referred to as Duchy, although the German Bund collapsed in 1866. Nevertheless, the Queen's Commissioner in Limburg is today still also referred to as Governor.

The multinational character of Limburg prior to these "recent" events that formed the current Dutch province of Limburg is evident in historical maps. Since the Middle Ages, the region has been a patchwork of cities and jurisdictions belonging to many fiefs, empires, federations, dioceses, duchies, counties, principalities and republics.

Beyond doubt, and to as great an extent as any region in Europe (and more than most), the region's relationship with borders has been historically dynamic. Popular belief is that, as a result, Limburg can still be characterised as being on the border between Germanic and Latin Europe, personified by both a northern rationally efficient lifestyle and a southern Burgundian one, on the fence between beer and wine, or oil and butter. As such an internationally contested region, Limburg has had several major impacts on European history:

- The Treaty of Meerssen was a partition treaty of the Carolingian Empire concluded on 8 August 870 by the two surviving sons of Emperor Louis the Pious, King Charles the Bald of West Francia and Louis the German of East Francia, at Meerssen, north of Maastricht, in present-day Limburg.
- Hendrik van Veldeke (in German: Heinrich von Veldeke), who was born before or around 1150 in Hasselt and wrote his first book in Maastricht, was the first writer in the Low Countries known by name to write in a European language other than Latin and had a tremendous impact on Germanic literary history.
- In January 1992, the European Union was established under the Treaty on European Union or so-called

Maastricht Treaty, further reuniting Europe after Limburg had played a significant role in dividing it in 870.

Nowadays Limburg retains its character as a unique border region. Not insignificantly, research into the functioning of urban networks as global hubs seems to suggest that cities in Limburg are part of the only polycentric functional urban area in Europe that spans three countries.[9] In fact, until the 1970s it was mandatory in schools in Limburg to learn French and German in addition to Dutch and English. The relaxation of this practice is now increasingly perceived as a roadblock to Limburg taking advantage of its Euregional embeddedness.

This could be summarised as a mantra for Limburg: we don't see borders, we see interfaces.

The Land of the Kazakhs

Table 6 categorises the various identity elements for the country of Kazakhstan. Based on the findings presented in Table 6, the identity of Kazakhstan seems to be made up of two broad categories. The pre-tsarist narrative of the nomadic tribes, the Kazakh Khanate and the steppe dominate the historic discourse. This is supplemented with the concept of cosmopolitan Kazakhstan as the cultural melting pot, linked to modern Almaty and Astana.

The historic discourse is characterised by perpetual nomadic mobility in the large open plains of the Steppe with a fluid – yet emotionally attached – concept of shared territory as a consequence. This is summarised in several Kazakh words that are seen to be central to the Kazakh cultural identity. *Kut berreke* expresses happiness, prosperity and riches through preservation, where *kut* (happiness) is linked to *this* land. *Paryz* refers to the indebtedness and responsibility the Kazakhs have towards future generations – hence the idea of taking responsibility for *this* land. *Namys* means honour; everything that is considered highly moral and worthy in a person. This is also used in greeting another person, as in *namisi bar*, which means "to have the honour". The combined quality of these identity markers and their significance today is exemplified by the omnipresent use of the *shanyrak* (yurt) as a symbol and reinforced by the national language policy.

Ethnic and international mobility is the essence of the cosmopolitan modern Kazakh identity. This outward looking open internationalism is illustrated by the president's initiatives in organising the Congress of World and Traditional Religions and in the policies of nuclear disarmament and the hosting of the OSCE summit & EXPO 2017.

Both these perspectives as described above have caused the Kazakhstani to be tolerant and diplomatic. They are tolerant, as in "open-minded towards the other" as opposed to "tolerating others", i.e. a co-habitation in peace. They are diplomatic in being receptive to novelty and the unusual. The use of soft power is preferred over hard power, also considering the geo-political location of the country. At the same time young Kazakhs are ambitious and eager to learn and succeed in a world that they are open to, outward looking and ready to discover. Hence the importance of 'the global dialogue of religions and civilizations', 'the cult of learning and education, as an intellectual foundation of the nation' and 'promoting the idea of peace and harmony', as expressed in the Patriot Act, *Mangilik Yel.*

This could be summarised as: to be patriotic is to be cosmopolitan.

Table 6: Constructive elements of Kazakhstani identity

Structural static elements (origins)	
History	Geography
The idea of nomadic tribes with no concept of territory is combined with the cultural melting pot	

Semi-static elements		
Greatness	Physical appearance	Mentality of the people
The Kazakh Khanate	The Steppe	Tolerance, forgiveness., mobility, fluidity, *kut* (happiness), *bata* (blessing by family elder over material gain), *namys* (honour); *paryz* (indebtedness)
Cosmopolitan Kazakhstan	Modern Astana	

Signifiers		
Great events/heroes	Food/architecture/arts/literature/popular culture	Language/traditions/ritual/folk
Ablai Khan fighting the Zhungars (Nomad movie)	*Beshbarmak, kumiss, akyns, dombra,* yurt	Nauryz festival Kokpar About 800 associations represent almost 50 ethnic groups, 23 native languages
Nazarbayev building Astana	Astana architecture	

Colouring elements		
Symbols	Behaviour	Communication
Eagle, shanyrak	Language policy	Crossroads of civilisations Heart of Eurasia Kazakh nationalism
Congress of World and Traditional Religions	Nuclear disarmament Hosting OSCE & EXPO	

Uprooted Dubai

In our 2009 volume[6], Frank M. Go and I identified some of the elements of the place identity of Dubai. First, the narrative of the nation seems to revolve around the history of the Bani Yas tribe of the UAE and the part of the Al Bu Falasah subsection that has been ruling Dubai since 1833 – the Al Maktoum family. The foundational myth seems to incorporate two elements: Bedouin life in the desert on the one hand; and pearling, the building of *dhows* and trading which centred around the Creek on the other. The latter element has had a dominant influence on the character of Dubai, as it splits the city in half. Some even suggest that the Creek is responsible for giving Dubai its name. An important socio-cultural tradition is found in Arab hospitality in general and in particular in the role of the *majlis*, as a place where men meet and discuss politics and decide on future directions, even today. Other traditions often referred to and still practised today are falconry, calligraphy, poetry, song writing (language), and men dancing along with the traditional *liwa* bands. Henna body painting, the use of perfume and incense burning is practiced primarily by women. One of the most important artefacts that gave Dubai its historical architectural character is the *baadgeer*, the wind tower that dominates rooftop views over historic parts of the city. Invented traditions include the public celebrations now held during Eid holidays, national day and festivals, and events in the restored historical quarters of the heritage village around HH Sheikh Saeed's House and the Bastakiya. As far as the original population of Dubai – the Emirati people – is concerned, their identity is largely determined by their religion, their position in the Middle East and their traditional attire still worn today. But at the same time it is these elements that also determine the West's prejudiced view of the region.

Imported traditions like belly dancing (mainly for tourists) and the tremendous investments in iconic projects appear to fill a void left by colonialism. These developments exert cultural power and thereby rapidly change the people and geography of Dubai. The growth in foreign direct investment, trade and tourism has led to a tremendous import of foreign labour, as well as technology. In a very short period of time, the local population has been rapidly forced to deal with elements of modernity while maintaining traditions. An interesting example of this is the adoption of mobile technology and instant messaging, in which Arabic script, emoticons, phonetic Arabic using Latin letters and numerals, and English words are used interchangeably.[10] Other issues raised by economic growth, internationalisation and tourism are concerned with the economic and employment positions of the local Emirati as well as environmental concerns. More specifically related to tourism, prostitution, the availability of alcohol and imbalances in cultural norms between hosts and guests might become issues in future.

Taking the above observations together, it seems that the obvious success of Dubai can be summarised as being a global business and tourism hub with a respect for tradition, heritage and local culture, where reputation is built through bold action, with mega-projects that are very often based on a vision anchored in this local identity. However, whether this concerted effort can be sustained with the level of development and import of investment, talent, tourism and trade currently taking place, is questionable. There are signs, as illustrated above, that the link with the identity of the community is weakening.

The Hague: City of Peace and Justice

Born as a royal hunting lodge in 1230, The Hague has been the political centre of the Low Countries for centuries. While the former European empires boasted undisputed capitals like London, Paris or Vienna, in which all political, economic and social-cultural power was concentrated in one grand place, the situation in the Netherlands was and is somewhat different. Amsterdam is now the country's official capital and the preferred location for corporate headquarters, but was and is not the seat of the Dutch government. Rotterdam is the centre for industry and logistics and the second-largest city in the country. The Hague is only third, yet it was and is the undisputed centre for affairs of state, the crown and diplomacy. Not being burdened by the pollution and turmoil of industry and trade, while located along the sandy North Sea beaches, The Hague has long been a welcome station for diplomats and a preferred destination for elites, envoys and international conferences. This has given the city a cosmopolitan character and elegance.

Hence, it is not really surprising that the Russian Tsar Nicholas II chose the somewhat neutral city of The Hague as the location for the first ever global peace conference, which was held in the year 1899 among 26 participating nation states. The opening of the Peace Palace in 1913 was one of the subsequent milestones in the history of the city. Not only does it house the Permanent Court of Arbitration that was established as a result of the 1899 peace conference, but, as is often reported in the media, The Hague has also hosted the International Court of Justice since 1922 and the International Criminal Court since 2002.

In 1993 Boutros Boutros Ghali, at the time Secretary-General of the United Nations, stated that 'The Hague is the legal capital of the world'. Today in The Hague, over 19,500 individuals in some 160 international organisations work towards a common goal: a just and peaceful world. Since 2012, the city has been authorised by royal decree to carry the words "peace and justice" in its coat of arms.

2.3 Our shared values

Community identities are usually built on an underlying sense of morality, virtue or ethics. Considering that community identities are imagined by the members of the community and purposefully built by elites, the church and courts, moral virtue obviously grants legitimacy. France is built on the idea of *liberté, égalité, fraternité;* American freedom and opportunity on the idea that all men are created equal, that they are endowed by their 'creator with certain unalienable rights, that among these are life, liberty and the pursuit of happiness' ('give me your tired, your poor, your huddled masses yearning to breathe free'). Dubai established itself as a regional sanctuary of open-mindedness and diversity, the Dutch city of The Hague as the city of peace and justice (as illustrated above). Germany's *Gründlichkeit* is built on the virtue of hard work. Kazakhs tread lightly on the earth; London and New York City embrace diversity, Bhutan happiness and the Cantonese loyalty.

Unsurprisingly, it is this underlying ethical system that builds not only the imagined community, but also the way in which such communities accumulate global admiration. This is the conclusion I came to when I correlated the Good Country Index with the Anholt-GfK Roper Nation Brands Index™ (see Figure 1). One is a measure of countries' reputations, the other of their actual contribution to humanity and the planet.

Both indexes are brainchildren of Simon Anholt, independent policy adviser and author of *Competitive Identity* and *Places* among many other publications. Through my long collaboration with Simon I have been involved in building or analysing both indexes. The Anholt-GfK Roper Nation Brands Index™ is a large-scale opinion poll that surveys people's perceptions of other countries (see also Section 5.3). The survey has run annually since 2007 in about twenty panel countries, sampling 20,000 respondents representing 60 per cent of the world's population and 77 per cent of its economy. Respondents are asked to express their attitude towards 50 target countries on Likert scales grouped in six categories (exports, governance, investment and immigration, tourism, people, and culture and heritage). The survey asks questions like: 'I would buy products from there (exports dimension); I would like to have a friend from there' (people dimension); or 'that country offers natural beauty' (tourism dimension). By adding up all the scores on these various dimensions, an overall ranking is produced as presented in Figure 1. In 2014 the top three countries were Germany, the United States and the United Kingdom.

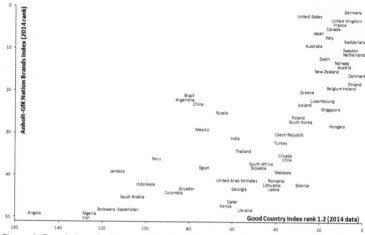

Figure 1: Correlation plot between the Good Country Index and the Anholt-GfK Roper Nation Brands Index™

Where the Anholt-GfK Roper Nation Brands Index™ measures perception, the Good Country Index measures reality in terms of how much countries contribute to humanity and the planet relative to their size as measured in US$ GDP. It is based, to a large extent, on United Nations system data sources that gauge countries' actual performance in seven categories: global contribution to science and technology, contribution to global culture, contribution to global peace and security, contribution to world order, contribution to planet and climate, contribution to global prosperity and equality, and contribution to global health and wellbeing. Each category contains five indicators, ranging from the number of Nobel prizes won (science and technology dimension) and exports of cultural goods (culture dimension) to number of peace troops contributed to UN missions (peace and security dimension) and pharmaceutical exports (health and wellbeing dimension). Most indicators are divided by each country's GDP to create a level playing field. Based on the average rank for all 35 indicators, Figure 1 shows that in 2014 the Netherlands contributed most to humanity and the planet per US$ GDP, followed by Switzerland, Denmark and Finland. Contrary to the Anholt-GfK Roper Nation Brands

Index™ (which is a commercial product), the Good Country Index is completely open source and can be accessed via www.good.country.

The countries that are included in both indexes are mapped on the two indexes in Figure 1. It is clear that there is a high level of correlation (80 per cent). This means that countries that are most admired usually also contribute more to humanity and the planet per US$ GDP (or limit their negative impacts). In other words, it seems that if communities want to be admired they have to behave (and let us hope that the reverse argumentation is also true; that admired countries are more likely to behave appropriately internationally, creating a virtuous circle). Figure 1 also seems to make clear, though, that some countries get more reputational value for their relative contributions than others. For instance, the United States, Brazil, Argentina, China and Russia are outliers to the left of where most countries are, which means that they score relatively high in the Nation Brands Index, compared to what they seem to be "entitled to" considering their score in the Good Country Index. The opposite is true for countries like the Netherlands, Denmark, Finland, Ireland or Hungary that get much less reputational value for the contributions that they make. The difference between these two clusters is of course size. Large countries, because of their impact in absolute terms, are more visible and more likely to be admired for what they do. Hence, for communities to be imaginative in the way that they do the things they do is particularly important for smaller communities. Why this is and how it is done will be addressed in the chapters that follow.

But as globalisation nibbles away at the edges of the imagined community and local identity is under pressure, is what surfaces possibly the moral virtue of humanity and the aim of contributing to the maintenance of universal values? And if it is not the church, the sacral monarchy or governments (at all levels) that provide us with guidance, are universal values then the last resort in a globalised world?

Figure 1 seems to support this assumption and we can see that this is already starting to take effect. World heritage sites are being recognised for their reputational value. The Chinese have decided to save the giant pandas in Chengdu, Sichuan and value them as powerful mesmerising mediators in international public diplomacy. The city of Amsterdam funded an imaginative lighting art event that saw the museum square drowned in laser lights to create an artificial underwater effect to build awareness of global warming and rising sea levels.

Maybe virtue has always been what united us and resulted in admiration, but in a globalised world it becomes even more important. Infusing that with local identity is part of the challenge; to tackle the paradox between global relevance and authentic community distinctiveness, or, vice versa, how local identity can be made to appeal to universal values. These challenges and how to address them will be covered in the following chapters.

Chapter 3
How we fight boredom: Community imagination

Imagination is its own form of courage and communities need lots of it in order to stand out.

In the context of this book I define imagination as the ability to construct mental visions of alternative realities based on information about current events and past experiences, perceptions and beliefs stored in memory. One would expect this to be a vital skill in today's world that is rapidly changing and challenged by accelerating global issues. It is fundamental to our ability to come up with new solutions and exciting initiatives that are world changing. We have never been in a better position to exploit this human quality than we are today. With artificial intelligence, computer simulation and augmented reality, we now have the ability to integrate the real and the virtual in order to visualise our imaginary worlds for prototyping and testing. Yet, it seems as though we are doing exactly the opposite, demanding safe and proven solutions, accountability and measurement, prudence and caution; sticking to the norms. This leads to copy-and-paste behaviour and boring leadership; people afraid to stick their neck out. Only those with sufficient courage or naivety will try something new or extraordinary. Yet, the latter is required in order to advance communities and to stand out. If that is done by matching community identity and global values persistently, it could lead to a long-term sense of direction as well as admiration. As Albert Einstein said, 'Imagination ... is more important than knowledge. Knowledge is limited. Imagination encircles the world.'

3.1 How we use our imagination

The World Values Survey[3] asks respondents around the world which child qualities are most important to them. The options are independence, hard work, responsibility, imagination, prudence, determination, perseverance, religious faith, unselfishness, obedience and self-expression. Generally, the one quality that we all value most in our children is imagination. This is followed by self-expression and unselfishness. The least important qualities in children are seen to be responsibility and hard work. Why is it that as we grow up, these priorities seem to be completely reversed? Particularly from those in leadership positions – managers, politicians, policy makers – we expect responsibility, hard work and prudence (accountability). Job descriptions rarely demand people with imagination. Yet, it is an essential quality in today's globalised and fast-paced society.

To come up with imaginative creations is to take our knowledge and personality and invent fantastic new ideas that are captivating. Imagination is about asking the question: what if? To imagine alternative routes, solutions and interpretations. What happens when we lack imagination is that new information is bent towards our preconceived ideas in order to confirm them. With a rich network of perceptions and beliefs we make sense of a complex world without constantly changing our mind. In other words, imagination is the catalyst for empathy, open-mindedness, tolerance and progress. Needless to say, in an environment of cultural diversity, this is even more important. Hence, for communities to acquire positioning on the global playing field, imagination is the key.

What I am referring to, of course, is imagination as a community activity. If ideas remain locked up in one person's mind, they are useless. Therefore, even though leadership is important, as leaders can set the tone, encouraging communities and stakeholders to ask questions and engage in an exchange of ideas and ideation is essential. Collaboration is therefore just as important as strong leadership. It is about looking at what we have from different religious, cultural and disciplinary perspectives in order to come up with something new and imaginative, so as to keep identity alive; to take stakeholders out of their comfort zone and challenge their perspectives and skills in order to reach for the extraordinary; the next level of development.

Florence

The earliest manifestations of the European Renaissance emerged in Florence in the fifteenth century. It is often referred to as the rebirth of imagination. As one of the Italian city states, Florence acquired economic prominence by providing credit to European monarchs and inventing the banking system. The leading family in Florence for three centuries and responsible for much of the Italian Renaissance was the House of Medici. In particular, Cosimo de' Medici (1389–1464) and his heirs used their vast fortune and newly acquired political control to sponsor the revival of education, the arts and architecture. It was partly possible because of the stability brought about through international relations and treaties.

In 1444, Cosimo de' Medici founded the first public library in support of the humanist movement. Cosimo commissioned Donatello's famous *David* and Ficino's Latin translation of the complete works of Plato (the first ever translation). Other notable Medici protégés were Michelangelo and Leonardo da Vinci.

Most notably, Cosimo facilitated architect Brunelleschi to complete the dome of the Cattedrale di Santa Maria del Fiore in 1436. The Duomo was the largest in the world and to this day remains the largest brick dome ever constructed. The plans for the dome were thought to be unachievable because of the sheer size and height, while services in the church were not to be interrupted during construction. Yet, Brunelleschi's solutions were such that with unparalleled progressive ingenuity, intuition and imagination he constructed something that, in terms of understanding of physics and maths, was centuries ahead of its time. It is probably one of the first examples of captivating and imaginative iconic masterpiece structures built to attract visitors to the city.

Oslo

If there is any project that is largely imagination, it is Oslo's *Future Library*. In 2015, the city wanted to exemplify its positioning as a young pioneering city. It decided to fund Scottish artist Katie Paterson's 100-year artwork, *Future Library*. Paterson planted 1,000 trees just outside Oslo to supply paper for a special anthology of books to be printed in 100 years' time. In the meantime, each year, one author contributes a manuscript, which is held in a trust, unpublished, until 2114, to reflect the city's forward-looking mentality and mantra that the best is yet to come. In the meantime, the manuscripts will be held in a specially designed room in the New Oslo Public Library, due to open in 2019. They will be on display, but not available for reading.

The prizewinning author, poet and essayist Margaret Atwood was named as the first writer to contribute to the project. On 26 May 2015 she handed over her manuscript at a public event in the newly planted forest, followed by interviews in the library. This event briefly grabbed the world's attention. 107 million people were reached worldwide through social media, and editorial coverage in the likes of *The New York Times*, the BBC, *The Huffington Post*, CTV News, *The Observer*, *Argentina Star*, *Aktif Medya* and *The Post Internazionale* reached 4 million people.

Nurturing the forest and ensuring its 100-year preservation is counterbalanced in the invitation extended to each writer: to conceive and produce a work in the hope of finding a receptive reader in an unknown future. This, more than anything, requires imagination. Oslo's *Future Library* might not be a useful library for the citizens of Oslo today. Nor is it a major attraction for tourists or an appealing opportunity for investors. However, it has created a forest that is more than just another forest and books that are more than just new books. It creates anticipation and, most importantly, captivates audiences by stimulating curiosity.

3.2 How we use real and virtual

Where imagination enhances our sensory information to imagine alternative realities based on our cognition and fantasies, the same can be done by linking the real with the virtual. Augmented and virtual reality promises to provide tremendous opportunities for imaginative communities, as they allow for the creation of alternative and captivating experiences that build local character, engagement and recognition, through technology and online distribution. Imagine how many kids and young adults know their way around Los Angeles perfectly, without ever visiting, but by playing hours and hours of *Grand Theft Auto 5* on their game consoles.

Today, for instance, the Berlin Wall is back. Wondering what it would have been like to live in Berlin and have this gigantic concrete wall blocking your way? You can now find out as it is possible to walk through the streets of Berlin and revisit history by projecting the wall that once divided West Berlin from East Germany onto what are now open public spaces, using an augmented reality app on your mobile device. The wall was torn down in 1989, but is now back in its original geographical context in Berlin with the Berlin Wall 3D app, built on the Layar augmented reality platform.

Similarly, it is possible to walk through historical sites like the Coliseum, Forum and Parthenon in Rome and experience them in their former glory by mixing reality with 3D reconstructed virtual environments, using tracking and location data on your mobile device or goggles. 'It is almost like entering a time machine', according to the Hermes Virtual Tour, which is built on the Wikitude platform.

Conversely, without ever going there, it is possible to experience other places online in virtual worlds such as Second Life or through immersive virtual tours using 360 degrees and 3D video-recording and playback technology. To some it might sound futuristic, but it is in fact widely available for anyone with access to YouTube or other common platforms.

We can use the connection between real and virtual, online and offline, to engage with external audiences and to enhance their engagement with our communities. It provides a whole new landscape for imaginative community initiatives that reconstruct identities, modernise and contextualise them or build new ones while engaging publics. One of the first countries to build its strategy on this idea is Estonia.

Estonia

The country has been invaded and occupied so many times over the course of its history that on independence from the Soviet Union in 1991 Estonians must have thought there was no point in hanging on to physical borders; in twenty years they built the most advanced e-state in the world. Part of what drove this push for a "digital republic"[11] was the fact that Skype was invented and built in Estonia. Now, common government services such as education, health care, elections, the legal system, taxation and others are digitally connected on one single platform; and, if everything is in "the cloud" one can run a borderless state.

This has caught the world's attention, starting with, in 2001, Estonia being one of the first countries to declare internet access a human right. However, what has really captivated foreign audiences is the launch of a programme called e-residency. According to the official e-estonia.com website, 'E-Residency is a new digital nation for global citizens, powered by the Republic of Estonia. It is a transnational digital identity that can provide anyone anywhere with the opportunity to succeed as an entrepreneur. Like citizens and residents of Estonia, e-residents receive a government-issued digital ID and full access to Estonia's public e-services. This enables them to establish a trusted EU business with all the tools needed to conduct business globally. They can then use their secure digital identity to manage their company entirely online from anywhere in the world with minimal cost and hassle.' As of 1 June 2018, 33,438 people from 154 countries had applied to set up 5,033 companies.

With the Estonian government in the cloud, another brilliant imaginative initiative is the establishment of data embassies. The idea is that state-owned server resources are located outside the country's territorial borders, but remain under its control. This is possible because of the fact that embassies have immunity and are protected under international law. Estonia opened its first data embassy in the Grand Duchy of Luxemburg in late 2017 and others will be added. These server resources are capable not only of providing data back-ups, but also of operating the most critical e-services for the country. It makes it possible for the Estonian state to continue operating under conditions where its local data centres have been stopped or disturbed due to a natural disaster, large-scale cyber-attack, power failure or other crisis situation.

3.3 How we match values

Imaginative initiatives have to engage both the local community and international audiences. They have to be communicative across cultures, social groups and lifestyles; hence the idea of value matching – high-level positioning – is essential. So really it is about matching community values with universal human values.

In advertising the golden rule is that messages should have any one or more of three types of appeal: emotional, rational or moral. Rational appeals address the audience's self-interest at the level of cognition (i.e. logical mental processing and reasoning). Emotional appeals stir up positive or negative sentiments at the level of affection. Positive emotional appeals might include love, humour, fun or pride. Negative emotional appeals can relate to fear, guilt or shame. Lastly, moral appeals address our sense of right and wrong.

One of the reasons why imaginative initiatives are engaging is because they often unite these various types of appeals in such a way that mass audiences understand the underlying universal values (morally, rationally and emotionally). Florence's Renaissance project was rational in terms of human and economic development, emotional in its aesthetics and moral in its religious foundation. Oslo's *Future Library* is rational in its contribution to knowledge and culture, emotional in its love towards future generations and moral in its conservation. Estonia's e-residency is rational in its effective and efficient use of technology, emotional as it is intriguing and moral as it seems to advocate open borders.

Bhutan

A country folded away for centuries in the Himalayan wrinkles between India and China suddenly captured the world's attention towards the end of the twentieth century. It challenged existing ideas of what it meant to join the global order entering the twenty-first century, literally and figuratively. On ascending the throne in 1972, the fourth ruler of Bhutan, King Jigme Singye Wangchuck, set out to redefine third-millennium prosperity and the terms on which he would open up his country's economy. As the Washington Consensus continued to propagate gross national product and economic growth as the yardsticks for development and prosperity, the new king advanced the idea of gross national happiness. It would prove to be an idea whose time had come.

To some it may now sound like lucky and clever public relations rhetoric, but for many Bhutanese it is both a utopian philosophy and a practical guiding principle. Gross national happiness is based on four principles: sustainable development, environmental conservation, preservation and promotion of cultural values, and good governance. The Gross National Happiness Commission is charged with implementing the concept in Bhutan. It has resulted in tangible imaginative initiatives.

One specific policy that has not gone unnoticed is that while most countries subsidise tourism in order to attract visitors from abroad, Bhutan actually imposes a rule that tourists must book their trip through a licenced Bhutanese tour operator and that a US$200 per day (low season) and US$250 per day (high season) minimum package applies. Included in this price is a US$65 per day Sustainable Development Fee that goes towards free education, free health care and poverty alleviation. In other words, tourists are taxed significantly as a result of the government's strict 'high-value, low-impact tourism' policy that protects the country's culture, traditions and natural environment while benefitting local development.

The idea of gross national happiness also resulted in a happiness index, global gross national happiness conferences, and a Centre for Bhutan Studies and GNH Research in Thimphu. Some doubt whether the gross national happiness drive has really pushed Bhutan into the twenty-first century, as most of the country's population still lives in poverty. Others argue that it has functioned as propaganda to hide internal ethnic conflicts. Undeniably though, gross national happiness has had an impact on the global reputation of Bhutan, as the idea has really caught on internationally – rationally, emotionally and morally.

United States of America, land of the free

Probably the noblest experiment to build a grand imaginative community based on virtue must be the United States of America.

Already during colonial times, in the seventeenth century, the poor, the oppressed and the entrepreneurial moved across the Atlantic from the "old world" for the promise of a better life, freedom and opportunity in the new one. It was primarily England that formed the new world in terms of language, morals and manners, but minority groups of settlers from across Europe joined in: the Dutch in New Amsterdam, along the Hudson River, and in New Jersey and Delaware; Swedes along the Delaware River; Germans in Pennsylvania; and Scots and Irish everywhere. The Pilgrim Fathers, orthodox Protestants fleeing England to escape the perceived tyranny of the Church of England, settled in the North hoping to build a theocratic prototype Kingdom of God. It was to be a harmonious society: a shining city on a mountain, to use biblical terms. They sowed the seeds for American idealism, even if it was to be a secular one.

This idealism became more pronounced during the struggle for independence from the British Empire. In January 1776, in a pamphlet entitled *Common Sense*, journalist Thomas Paine wrote about the prospect of a new nation; a last refuge for those who wanted to be free. 'O! ye that love mankind! Ye that dare oppose not only the tyranny but the tyrant, stand forth! Every spot of the old world is overrun with oppression. Freedom has been hunted round the globe. Asia and Africa have long expelled her. Europe regards her as a stranger, and England has given her warning to depart. O! receive the fugitive and prepare in time an asylum for mankind.' On these kinds of big uplifting words America is built; but what a task, what an immense dream to aim for.

It was to be the essence of the Declaration of Independence, written by Thomas Jefferson and endorsed on the fourth of July, Independence Day. The classic lines are of course that 'we hold these truths to be self-evident, that all men are created equal, that they are endowed by their Creator with certain inalienable rights, that among these rights are life, liberty and the pursuit of happiness'. The new country was soon to be recognised by many states and the first ever American embassy anywhere in the world was opened in the city of The Hague in 1782 (see the case study on The Hague in Chapter 4).

The declaration aimed to be a justification, a message to the world explaining why the Americans were embarking on this great adventure. The promise of America was a promise to humanity and was to be understood as such by people around the world. It was, at the time, devoid of nationalist sentiment. The declaration was intended as a global standard for a free society – known, honoured and admired by all – to constantly aim for, never to be perfectly achieved, but to approximate ever more closely, so as to increase and intensify its influence and bring happiness and hope to all people of all colours everywhere. This is the way in which Abraham Lincoln explained Jefferson's words 80 years later.

Lincoln would do everything to maintain that promise and the American unity in freedom during the civil war in the second half of the nineteenth century. In his famous speech on the battlefield of Gettysburg (19 November 1863) he explained that the war was needed to defend the new nation 'conceived in liberty and dedicated to the proposition that all men are created equal ... that we here highly resolve that these dead shall not have died in vain; that this nation, under God, shall have a new birth of freedom, and that the government of the people, by the people, for the people, shall not perish from the earth'.

Needless to say, since those early days, migrants and refugees from around the world have poured into the USA to contribute to the effort to build a free society, the mythology of cowboys and the Wild West – and the right to bear arms – being exemplary. Yet, it was not without its challenges. During two world wars in the first half of the twentieth century it would struggle with its international role as the enforcer of freedom and democracy. John F. Kennedy would answer to the global expectations regarding America's role in the world; in fact, he would awaken them. He spoke of a New

Frontier with unlimited possibilities and opportunities, citing the old Puritan call to build the biblical city on the hill in the new world. And if that was not enough, America should not only be an example; it should lead the world into a better future. 'Let every nation know, whether it wishes us well or ill, that we shall pay any price, bear any burden, meet any hardship, support any friend, oppose any foe, in order to assure the survival and success of liberty.' This would also compel Kennedy to finally deal with the civil rights of blacks, which had been a festering open wound in American society for centuries, incompatible with American idealism.

What the civil rights struggle also showed is that if there is any way in which America is unique, it is probably the way it is gifted with the ability to thoroughly incriminate itself[12]. It is an essential characteristic of American civil society, but also the private sector; news agencies taking on the battle for freedom of the press; Google and Apple fighting for freedom of information; and every time, Hollywood joins in. As a result, America's challenges have always been taken on publicly, out in the open and on an international scale. It has shown the world that it has been difficult to reconcile idealism with materialism (an ideal society under God, versus technical progress, consumerism and capitalism), to understand its role in the world (such as in Latin America, Korea or Vietnam) or to decide on how to treat Native Americans.

Today, the USA is struggling with the question of how to deal with immigration and globalisation. It is not surprising that large populations in America, but even more vigorously elsewhere, are so frustrated with the Trump administration as it is disowning the shining city on the hill, denying humanity the centuries-old promise of a better world. However, history has shown that whatever its challenges, this imaginative community of determined individuals is very likely to ultimately rediscover its virtue.

Chapter 4
How we become admired: Imaginative communities

Admired communities create amazing imaginative stuff that is uniquely befitting, built on collaboration and engagement.

Imaginative communities with a strong sense of belonging and calling can acquire international admiration when they implement projects, infrastructures, policies, investments or events that fit their character and are internationally relevant. By doing amazing stuff that makes a real global contribution such communities can enchant foreign audiences. Original, creative and engaging initiatives are communicative in their own right and hence, in today's media landscape, can generate their own reach through social media and subsequent mainstream media reporting. By focusing on initiatives that are befitting and hence addressing or questioning existing beliefs and media coverage, impacts can be enhanced. At the same time, it allows for more effective and efficient stakeholder involvement. Communities with a sense of direction are better able to bring together public, private and civil society stakeholders, as they feel part of a shared purpose. This, in turn, dramatically enhances the capacity for communities to produce imaginative ideas and creations. As a virtuous circle this reinforces the sense of a shared vision and the community's long-term ability to captivate. It almost becomes a way of life that operates at a level independent from political cycles or short-term challenges.

4.1 How we construct

Chapter 2 has shown that in order to be admired, communities need to contribute to humanity and the planet. It is actions that build reputations, not words. Hence, to enhance or change reputation is to construct infrastructures, projects, policies or events that contribute to the community, but also to humanity and the planet at large. Communities need to look at what they are good at, what fits their identity and what the local aspirations are, in order to make sure that initiatives have a local "signature" and are recognisably "from somewhere". To copy and paste trophy simulacra buildings or events does not bring much benefit to anyone but the vanity of the leader or the owner who ordered it.

At the same time imaginative communities need to look at what is relevant in a global context. What is it that is important and befitting to the community that is also pertinent to people elsewhere? Imaginative communities need to understand how they are currently being perceived and talked about by outsiders in order to address preconceived ideas and to attach new meaning to existing clichés and stereotypes. This is looked at in more detail in Chapters 5 and 6.

To be captivating is to create mesmerising and enriching experiences. The natural channels through which communities engage with the outside world are travel and tourism, cultural exchange, trade, investment, migration (via diaspora as well as immigration), education, science and technology exchange, diplomacy and public diplomacy, sports and popular culture. These are all areas in which there are opportunities to create imaginative community initiatives, enriching encounters that people will remember and share. This is the domain of imagineering, as will be discussed in more detail in Chapter 7.

Landscape, cityscape, architecture, conservation, revitalisation and spatial planning are important disciplines in this area as they alter reality but are communicative at the same time. The physical landscape provides clues about the identity of place in its geography, climate, history, development, change in physical appearance and the mentality of the community. In short, it informs the 'sense of place'. Landscapes' imageability (ability to generate images) provides clues for 'productisation' (e.g. as attraction) and representation; assigning meaning to place. Visual landscape allows for effective image projection and landscape as performance provides "ways of seeing" for consumption experience. All this facilitates landscape embodiment; for consumers to enrich their perceived image of place.

The Ancient Mediterranean

Ever since the first agricultural revolution and human settlement (since 10,000 BCE), people have had the urge to use their imagination in order to construct grand monuments that altered landscapes in glory and transmission of power, triumph, and religious justification and gratitude. The best architects, latest technologies, most fashionable designs and armies of highly skilled labour were used – a practice that has continued until today, not to own the latest, tallest or most expensive structure, but to reflect cultural significance, uniquely local capabilities and achievements, and to confirm (heavenly) power.

Some of the earliest man-made mega-structures are possibly the most significant illustration of this. Mark Lehner argues that as 'products of the land and people of Egypt's oldest kingdoms, in their pristine form the pyramids were the closest mankind has ever come in architecture to creating an illusion of transcending the human condition. Their aura of otherworldliness still inspires the popular imagination to seek their origin anywhere other than the people who inhabited the lower Nile Valley between five and three thousand years ago.'[13]

The outer casing of the pyramids was made of smoothed white limestone. Most of this valued glossy surface of most pyramids has since been stolen, but 45 centuries ago, when the pyramids were completed, their brilliance must have been blinding. The tallest pyramids, those of Giza, were built with slopes at an angle of roughly 50 degrees. Hence, at high noon, the reflection of the sun would illuminate much of the surrounding landscape, honouring the sun god in a most spectacular manner.

Of course, as we know, the pyramids were primarily built as tombs for the pharaohs. However, it was far more than just the grave of a king. One of the defining traits of the ancient Egyptian state and the legitimisation of its power was the tradition that the king was believed to be an incarnation of the god Horus. On the death of the king, the god transferred to the next sovereign and the dead king was – from then onwards – recognised and honoured as the divine father of Horus, Osiris. The pyramid complex was therefore also a temple complex in worship of this Horus-Osiris divinity, merged with the sun god Ra. But a pyramid complex was also a major economic engine, a catalyst for internal colonisation and the development of 'Egypt as one of the world's first true states. The complete pyramid played many roles: massive labour project; baker and brewer for hundreds of consumers; colonizer of the Egyptian provinces; employer of farmers, herdsmen and craftsmen of all kinds; temple and ritual centre at the core of the Egyptian state; reliquary of a king; embodiment of light and shadow; and the union of heaven and earth, encapsulating the mystery of death and rebirth.'[13]

The same can be said for the Forum Romanum, which largely had two functions: commercial-economic and political-religious. Yet, its meaning also developed, extended and changed from symbol of the republic's liberty and democracy to symbol and monument of the empire. The imperial forums are made up of many separate contributions and elements from different eras: all are impressive constructions and memorials representing the people of Rome and the empire in their own right. Even today, albeit in mutilated form, the Roman forums are representative of our own time and culture as it has emerged from the world of classical antiquity (even owing a lot of credit to the Greek Agora).

The most recent and – at the same time – largest imperial forum is that of Trajanus. As tradition demanded, this complex contained useful spaces for politics, governance, trade and education (the Auditorium), but its outspoken political message conveyed an ideological meaning: Trajanus, a great warlord and the first emperor to have been born in the province, as the bringer of peace – a freedom from strife that was imposed on Rome's enemies by Trajanus' heavy use of arms. The forums glorified emperors as military leaders and enlightened heads of state, but also represented cultural identity and, with the adjacent Coliseum, formed the backdrop to life in the city.[14]

As monuments, both the pyramids and the Roman forum have left humanity in awe at what it can achieve, considering that these mega-structures were created thousands of years ago.

Dubai

The United Arab Emirates, like many Arab countries, owe a lot of their development to one single tree: the date palm. It is widely recognised in the Arabian Gulf as the unique source of life. The date palm is believed to have been cultivated for over seven thousand years. The trunk of the tree stocks nutrients that allow it to resist drought and hence withstand high temperatures and harsh climatic conditions. In a desert region such as the Middle East the date palm tree has therefore provided a lifeline for its nomadic people. The tree provides shade, nutritional fruits and wood as building material, while the leaves and fronds are used to make baskets, ropes and medicine.

Hence, it is not surprising that the date palm tree is a regional symbol of importance. An old Arab proverb stating that 'the uses of the date palm are as many as the number of days in the year' can still be heard today. The Carthaginians depicted the date palm on coins and monuments. Israel's ten-shekel coin features a date palm. It is depicted in the coat of arms of Saudi Arabia. In Abu Dhabi the International Date Palm Festival is organised each autumn, and, as a symbol of abundance, dates are very popular in the Middle East for breaking the fast during Ramadan.

Hence, when the rulers of Dubai considered extending their coastline, the idea of creating artificial islands in the shape of date palm trees was clever. The palm tree shape with its many fronds allowed for the creation of lots of high-value beachfront property. At the same time, the symbolism was relevant and uniquely appropriate for the location of the islands in the Arabian Gulf. It was an imaginative idea which made sense from the perspective of communicability. If you are going to build artificial islands to add landmass, why not build them in the shape of something captivating?

The story goes that the imaginative palm island idea was dreamed up by Sheikh Mohammed Bin Rashid Al Maktoum, then crown prince and now ruler of Dubai. Sometime around the year 2000 engineers at the Dutch dredging consortium Van Oord received a phone call from Dubai asking them to meet with Sheikh Mohammed himself to discuss the feasibility of the project. There were no concrete plans, no local project engineers and no feasibility and potential impact studies (which raises the question whether, today, too many imaginative ideas and ambitious plans are suffocated by cost-benefit analyses).

The concept of a palm tree-shaped island made out of sprayed-on sand and protected by a seventeen-kilometre rocky crescent breakwater was designed and tested in large laboratory-type water basins in Rotterdam and Delft. Computer modelling was used to simulate the erosive impact of the currents and waves and estimate the impact of the project on the local and regional ecosystem. Van Oord commenced construction works for the first palm island, Jumeirah, in 2001 and residents began moving into the 4,000 villas and apartments at the end of 2006. By then, Nakheel, a real estate company and developer owned by the government of Dubai, was managing the island. The tree itself is mostly residential; the crescent boasts hotels and leisure facilities.

Beyond contributing economic opportunities, captivating experiences and an imagineering accomplishment – engineered for the imagination – the palm islands probably contribute little to humanity or the planet. In fact, the islands' environmental impact has been criticised. Nevertheless, with the local climate, the islands allow for great sea-sun-sand holiday and leisure experiences, amazing aerial photography and shareable content. They have grabbed the world's attention and mesmerised global audiences. A Google news search for "palm tree-shaped island" results in over 60,000 links to stories in the global news media.

4.2 How we communicate

Communities should stop paying to push messages down the throats of an unwilling international audience. Advertising or public relations are really not the way to build community reputation. While in the commercial world advertising might have a significant impact on consumer perceptions of goods, services and corporations and has a role to play in tourism, export or investment promotion, it plays a very limited role in the way that people build a mental map of "foreign" cities, regions and countries. In that context, personal experience, word of mouth – and more importantly nowadays, of course, social media – as well as mainstream news media play a much bigger role.

Through their purposeful actions imaginative communities set the media agenda, as opposed to having agenda setting push them into the corner. Unless they have a proactive approach to engaging with the media, creating stuff that sets the agenda, communities need public relations services, press officers, and strategic communication policies and procedures, all as reactive systems for damage control. Imaginative communities create stuff that journalists, online influencers, bloggers and locals (as online ambassadors) are eager to talk about and that provides shareable content, the kind of engaging buzz that people want to share on social media. This "action communication" is elaborated upon in Chapter 6. It is proactive and does not require spin.

Ideally communities should try to address existing clichés and stereotypes (see Chapter 5) by changing the perspective and finding creative and appealing ways to contradict them or, even better, light-heartedly poking fun at them with a hint of self-deprecation or humility. For instance, Europeans visiting Dubai are very surprised to find delightfully kind and helpful Emirati in national dress serving as hosts or customer assistants in hotels and the metro system. Such encounters are relatively rare – there are not many Emirati working in service jobs – but they are very powerful in changing preconceived perceptions of Arabs being formal, inaccessible and unfriendly. This is communicative in itself, but of course it does not reach many people directly. However, for those who do have this type of encounter, it could be mind changing and spark conversation. In addition, it probably leaves a very good impression among participants in familiarisation trips, trade missions and visits by foreign press.

Finland

Shareable content – light-heartedly poking a little fun at existing clichés – was provided by Finland's Ministry of Foreign Affairs in late 2015. The Finns were the first to come up with the idea of launching a unique set of text-messaging emojis or emoticons communicating typically Finnish feelings and customs. Many countries now offer their own sets of emojis – a cartoon-type language based on symbols like smileys – but Finland was the first country with its own official set of country emojis. The Finns received a lot of credit for their imaginative initiative, not least because the Finnish emojis include quirky icons of a head-banger, a sauna and the unbreakable classic Nokia 3310 mobile phone, icons that the world is familiar with. The initiative is reflective of the tech-savvy, quirky, fun-loving nature of the Finns. It is easy to recognise as typically Finnish considering Nokia invented text messaging in the first place.

Four of the Finnish emojis have been submitted for Unicode character standardisation, so they can be included in the official international emoji collection available for all devices. The Finnish emojis remain ever present, not just on keyboards, devices, apps or in mobile conversations, but also in physical form. They feature in *Trivial Pursuit* (the popular board game) questions, high-school books, scientific research, and on products such as t-shirts, reflectors and postcards.

The initiative received global attention. It was covered in over 2,000 news articles in 130 countries. On social media the story reached 300 million people worldwide (according to Meltwater social media analysis). The dedicated emoji keyboard app and images have been downloaded around 300,000 times and the project has received over twenty communications awards. The Finnish government itself acknowledges that the initiative was a success but only 'a small drop in the sea, hopefully leaving a tiny trace of a country that is easy-going and can laugh at itself and is technologically savvy'.[15]

4.3 How we collaborate

Imaginative communities find ways to bridge the gaps between community identity and its image internationally. This is done by

67

creating value-matched imaginative stuff and, by doing so, setting the media agenda. This cannot be done without collaboration. Communities are constructed by government, private sector and civil society at large. Together they create experience environments; places that people can visit, that produce exports, culture and events, and that provide investment opportunities and "a home". Imaginative communities are really networks that construct enchanting experiences for people to encounter each other. In Chapter 7 this is referred to as the "imagineering" of engagement by "experience networks".

This requires stakeholder collaboration which is not always easy to obtain and sustain. Public agencies, companies and associations all have their own interests and, very often, the reaction to the challenge of reputation management is to brag about individual achievements. Also, identity is usually contested and exploited for individual gain. Therefore, to find a common narrative and the collaborative spirit to join forces in community construction and its international projection is a considerably challenging task. Public versus private sector, government versus electorate, and the community versus outside observers, do not always see eye to eye and conflicting interests can be extremely demanding for the maintenance of a collaborative spirit.

To continue with examples from the Emirate of Dubai, in 2006 Sheikh Mohammed, on becoming ruler of Dubai, was confronted with a delicate conundrum. A 40-day period of national mourning was declared on the death of his brother, the previous ruler. Government offices were shut for seven days, a Fatboy Slim concert was cancelled and the Dubai marathon was put on hold. As usual, during the mourning period the consumption of alcohol and live music were also banned. This created a major problem for one of the large local hospitality companies, which was preparing to host thousands of employees of a major German firm on an incentive trip to Dubai, which included pop stars being flown in and, obviously, the usual alcoholic beverages. The need to continue international business as usual so as to avoid negative reputational impacts was clearly in conflict with local customs. It was agreed by the authorities, including Sheikh Mohammed himself, to move the whole event, including a new access road built by the municipality, into the desert, minimising impact on mourning locals. The "party in the desert" story is an interesting case of balancing local traditions with global reputational consequences. Of course, this kind of imaginative solution can only be accomplished in a collaborative spirit.

The Hague

The city that hosted the first ever global peace conference at the end of the nineteenth century, home of the peace palace and the United Nations courts has, unsurprisingly, chosen to designate itself "city of peace and justice". This positioning has become so successful that the phrase has taken on a life of its own and resulted in unexpected coalitions and initiatives that reinforce the city's standing.

In 2012 the Ministry of Foreign Affairs of the Netherlands (headquartered in The Hague) and the Municipality of The Hague initiated the Hague Peace and Justice Project. It collaborates with other Dutch government entities, international government organisations (such as the international courts and tribunals, but also over twenty other organisations), close to ten knowledge institutions, over 100 NGOs, media organisations and the private sector. The group organises joint outbound missions and visits to other countries for diplomacy and outreach, public dialogues in The Hague and elsewhere (the HagueTalks), and learning and training programmes.[16]

Each year on 21 September, the Just Peace festival takes place in the city of The Hague. Just Peace connects educational, cultural, international and non-governmental organisations that operate in The Hague and contribute to peace and justice, celebrating the annual United Nations peace day with over 40 activities including debates, concerts, performances and sports activities focused around the theme of peace and justice.

Like most cities, The Hague has its own innovation and start-up hub, but it is unlike most others in being aligned with the city's positioning. The Hague Security Delta accelerates collaboration in the Dutch security cluster, connects businesses, governments and knowledge institutions, and facilitates knowledge sharing between them. Together with partners it sets up innovation programmes which are open to all, establishes both national and international knowledge and trade partnerships, and provides access to markets, innovation, knowledge, capital and talent. All this is done to achieve a common goal of creating a more secure world, besides more business activity and more jobs. The Security Delta organises the Cyber Security Week events, and boasts a campus and a summer school.

Lastly, the Embassy of The Hague is a group of over 200 volunteers who provide hospitality services whenever the city hosts international events. City hosts and logistical staff help welcome foreigners to the city, providing them with information and support. Again, because of the collaboration of various organisations and the strong sense of community pride in the city, The Hague is able to make a mark. In the 2011 Anholt-GfK Roper City Brands Index™ this city of only half a million citizens is ranked 37th, just behind Beijing, Shanghai and Auckland.

Den Bosch

His paintings have travelled the world and are on display in Berlin, Bruges, Frankfurt, Ghent, Kansas City, Madrid, New York, New Haven, Paris, Rotterdam, Venice, Vienna and Washington, in world-renowned museums like the Louvre, Prado and the Metropolitan. None of his works are to be seen anywhere near his home town. Nevertheless, the city of Den Bosch (or 's-Hertogenbosch), in the south of the Netherlands, insisted that, in 2016, it wanted to commemorate the 500th anniversary of Hieronymus Bosch's death. It was a big aspiration with international allure for a relatively small city in a small country (Den Bosch has a population of roughly only 150,000 and is ranked seventeenth among Dutch cities according to number of inhabitants).

Yet, with Rembrandt, Van Gogh and Vermeer, Hieronymus (or Jeroen) Bosch is one of the most famous Dutch painters of all time and his reputation probably preceded that of the city by far. His most acclaimed work is *The Garden of Earthly Delights* which is housed in the Prado Museum in Madrid. Bosch made history as the "creator of devils" with his satirical creations and fantastical style. Pieter Brueghel the Elder was one of Bosch's most well-known followers.

So how could Den Bosch commemorate this painter, who was born in, lived in and died in the city that gave him his name, without owning any of his works? With the Bosch Year 2016 in sight, government, private sector, cultural, educational and research institutions came together in 2010 to set up the Foundation Jheronimus Bosch 500. Its total budget reached €28 million, of which only eight million was provided by the municipal government. €20 million was contributed by other public, private and civil society organisations like the provincial and national governments, the European Union, cultural and research funds as well as commercial sponsorships and estimated ticket sales. In other words, every euro invested by the municipal government was matched with 2.5 euros from other sources.

Almost half this budget (€ 12 million) was reserved for The Bosch Research and Conservation Project and its exhibition. The project would be the largest of its kind ever conducted on the oeuvre of a single painter. Twenty museums across Europe and North America participated in the project, obtaining research and conservation support in relation to the works of Bosch in their possession. In return, the works would be shipped to the city of Den Bosch on temporary loan.

Nineteen out of 20 of Bosch's drawings and seventeen out of 24 of his paintings were thus temporarily obtained. They were documented using infrared reflectography and ultra high-resolution digital macro photography, both in infrared and visible light. Nine paintings were restored; one painting and one drawing were finally attributed to Bosch, eliminating years of doubt; and two paintings previously credited to Bosch were judged not to have been painted by him after all. Obviously, this raised controversy and resulted in global media attention for the project. On conclusion of the research and conservation project all the works were brought together in a unique Bosch exhibition, *Visions of Genius*, attended by 421,700 visitors from 81 countries between February and May 2016.

The Bosch exhibition was at the heart of the celebrations, yet the remaining €16 million budget was spent on a multi-year cultural programme leading up to and including the many activities during the festive year. Over one hundred festivals and events were organised by or with the help of all sorts of clubs, associations, schools and artists. Hieronymus appeared in landmarks, street art, tourist attractions, canal cruises, outdoor projections, parades, lessons and talks, books, film, theatre, dance and musical performances, games and documentaries. The cultural programme resulted in 1.4 million visits, generating estimated consumer spending of €52 million in the city, meaning that every euro invested by the municipality produced an economic effect of €6.5 locally. More importantly, the value of the media coverage generated by Hieronymus Bosch 500 was estimated to exceed €47 million: €27.6 million nationally and €19.6 million internationally. Presumably, this has had a significant impact on international awareness of the city. Also, 900 city residents volunteered to act as hosts. 58 per cent of Den Bosch's residents indicated that the events enhanced their sense of pride in their city.

It is admirable how the Dutch city of Den Bosch was able to mobilise everything and everyone in 2016 and the preceding years in order to commemorate the death of Hieronymus Bosch with a "we can do it together" mentality. It shows that with collaboration wild imagination can be turned into a reality.

ROBERT GOVERS

Chapter 5
What they think: Imaginary communities

Admiration is only attained by those communities that are able to break down barriers of awareness, stereotypes and clichés.

Communities are imagined within, but they are also imaginary outside. What I mean by this is that most people in the world will never actually experience many other different and distant communities directly. They might hear about them through the diaspora, media or friends and relatives, but their image of those communities is largely built on "virtual" mentally processed information. Hence, admiration can only be achieved if communities are able to build international awareness of their existence and, subsequently, induce a positive image in online and offline media (including social media, obviously). In order to do that successfully communities need to understand the way in which global audiences learn and understand the world around them.

5.1 How they imagine

There are several ways people store information and hence construct images of other people and communities. The basic building block is a link between two concepts, a mental connection which is referred to as a belief or an association, e.g. Australians are friendly. Australia and/or Australians are also believed to be informal, warm and/or adventurous. This kind of spider network set of associations is referred to as a schema. The concept of adventure, of course, has its own associations, such as hardship, trekking or discovery. These networks are subsequently linked into schemata, or mind maps.

Through simple inferences (inserting new concepts into existing schemata) we make sense of what we experience by linking it to our existing beliefs. If we think of Australians as adventurous, we might infer that when we visit the country, we will experience ruggedness and sparsely populated remote areas, but possibly also backwardness or lack of high culture. Clearly, such inferences can result in misinterpretations. Routine and trite associations that are popular and habitual are referred to as clichés. These can be particularly problematic as they are hard to get rid of, while they are often outdated and have lost their originality and relevance through long overuse.

Clichés can be particularly persistent when we try to understand people and places, for which we tend to use shared standard sets of generalised associations, or schemata, as stereotypes (a packet of inferences about the personality traits or attributes of a whole community). Whenever we meet someone from outside our own community, we have a tendency to use these standard inferences to typecast them. It is then up to that person to disprove or confirm the preconceived ideas that we have, which usually results in expanding the complexity of the active schemata, reducing the persistency of stereotypes and disproving clichés. So by linking schemata to each other in complex networks of inferences, we simplify our cognitive processes. However, the price we pay is that an object or event can be distorted if the schema used to encode it does not quite fit.

Image is the set of associations and its holistic, or *gestalt*, representations. Members of a community or outsiders that have visited or are engaged with the community usually have rich mental maps with many nodes and linked associations. These associations can even be categorised on three dimensions. One dimension ranges from cognitive to affective; from perceptions based on knowledge of functional characteristics to those based on feelings. Another dimension ranges from holistic general associations to attribute-based ones, pertaining to the whole versus its parts. Examples of cognitive attribute-based associations of geographical places could be climate, infrastructure or cost of living. Cognitive holistic associations might relate to landscape or cultural diversity. Examples of affective attribute-based associations could be feelings of safety or friendliness, while affective holistic associations could relate to general feelings of atmosphere or comfort. Lastly, the third dimension varies from common to unique. Some associations, such as expensiveness, quality of infrastructure or climatic conditions, potentially apply to many communities. Other associations could be unique to one community, as the House of Windsor is to the British, or pizza to the Italians.

However, communities are generally unfamiliar to most non-members, so "outsiders" tend to have very simplified, clichéd and stereotypical ideas about them – certainly not as multidimensional as described above. I have seen this in my own research when I asked an online sample of over 1,000 respondents from across the globe to describe, in their own words, the image that they have of Dubai, a place they had never been to. Many respondents commented on the position of women in Muslim society, expressing their concern about women not being allowed to drive cars, not seeing any women in public or having to go veiled as a non-Muslim female tourist. None of these associations are factually applicable to the Emirate of Dubai, but they appear to be true to the respondents involved. What is likely to happen in the minds of these individuals is that they know very little about Dubai, apart from the fact that it is situated on the Arabian Peninsula and they project associations that they have with Saudi Arabia onto Dubai. Basically all countries in the region, for many citizens in the world, equate to oil, wealth, desert, camels, hot weather, Arab-Muslim culture, busy streets and souks – in the popular imagination a mix of Lawrence of Arabia and *1001 Nights*. Dubai as the fast-growing cosmopolitan global hub in the Middle East with shimmering towers and a luxurious tourism offering is only slowly starting to acquire a place in people's schemata. The same is true for a country like Kazakhstan, which is impacted by the "-stan" effect, by which Pakistan, Afghanistan, Turkmenistan, Tajikistan, Kirgizstan, Uzbekistan and Kazakhstan are all seen as war-torn and corrupt countries that are dealing with Islamic extremism, regardless of the achievements of individual communities.

Images that are made up of only a few associations are referred to as weak images. Perceptions, schemata or images subsequently have an effect on attitude, which is the evaluation of the image against personal motivations and value judgements. It determines the degree of positivity or negativity with which a person approaches "others" and hence informs behaviour. Hence, both weak as well as rich images can lead to positive or negative attitudes. In fact, considering the cliché vilified or romanticised stereotypes that are attached to many communities, weak images can easily be found at the extremes of positive or negative attitude. Rich images mostly result in positive or mild attitudinal responses as those people with rich schemata usually have direct experience with the community in question and are therefore better informed and nuanced.

All of these mechanisms are processes of awareness. Without consciousness and recognition, previously established schemata cannot be adjusted and – similarly – new schemata require consciousness and identification to be created. It also means that image is a very personal construct. Many associations are not just a description of the community, but of the relationship between the community and the perceiver. This is also referred to as image self-congruity or self-focus. This means that image is influenced by cultural and social background, as well as a person's psychological and personal characteristics. Generally, people in neighbouring communities have a much stronger awareness and richer image of their neighbours than most other people. Also, whether you perceive another community as wealthy, religious or friendly depends on your own cultural baggage, social status and motivations.

Image and reputation are often used as interchangeable concepts, but they are not. *The* image of a community does not exist, as images are personal constructs, influenced by the cultural, social and psychological characteristics of the perceiver. Reputation is how groups collectively perceive a community (the aggregate of multiple images), which includes people familiar with the community as well as media representatives. These are shared perceptions and average evaluations (i.e. both an aggregate image and an average attitude) by the general public, including somewhat informed groups and people with experience. Hence, reputation includes assessments of awareness (i.e. recognition or prominence). People can also form an image of reputation. It is perfectly conceivable for an elderly person travelling to Amsterdam to say: 'I know Amsterdam has a reputation as a city of sex, drugs and rock 'n roll, but I want to go there, because the image that I have includes associations with Rembrandt and Van Gogh'.

5.2 How they learn and perceive

So, people make sense of the world by linking sets of associations or beliefs in schemata. Sensory stimuli (i.e. information packets that we form based on what we see, hear, feel, smell or taste) are processed in people's minds by trying to link them up with existing networks of association that they have been building and filing in memory since early childhood, based on past information or their own imagination. Overall memory therefore reaches far beyond the original information provided by any stimuli at any particular moment in time. But luckily, not all stimuli are processed. If they were, most people would end up in a mental institution.

People limit information processing and selective learning by applying five filters.

1. In order for their senses to be activated, people need to be exposed to stimuli. If the television is on, but a group of children are playing tag, blocking sight and sound, exposure might be limited.
2. If exposed, one needs to be attentive, i.e. allocating processing capacity. If the children are not playing loudly, but instead, are asking whether they can invite their friends over, it might draw attention away from what is being broadcast on television. Whether people are attentive or not also depends on each individual's needs, motivations, attitudes and attention span.
3. The third filter that people apply is comprehension. When they have been exposed and attentive to stimuli, those stimuli have to be interpreted. People attach meaning to a stimulus by contextualising it in terms of existing knowledge. The question is whether the stimulus can be categorised using existing concepts stored in memory and whether or not existing associations linked to that concept contradict the new stimulus or not. Or, in other words, the question is whether gestalt processing of the schema will allow the new stimulus to be organised and combined into an enhanced or more complete meaningful whole (i.e. whether it fills in missing parts or contradicts existing associations). Whether this will happen depends on the individual's knowledge, motivations, involvement and expectations.

4. Whether people change their minds based on new information depends on acceptance. If new information is understood, it does not necessarily mean that it is accepted. If new information just confirms existing beliefs, it might be discarded; if it fills gaps in a meaningful whole, it is more likely to be accepted. Where new information is contradictory or opens up routes to new associations and inferences, it is less likely to be accepted unless strong rational, ethical or emotional arguments are provided for replacing existing beliefs or creating new ones.

5. Finally, if new information is understood and accepted it needs to penetrate the filter of retention, which involves the filing of information in long-term memory. This is more likely to be successful when using pictures, concrete words, self-references, mnemonic devices and repetition.

Over the last ten or twenty years or so, communities have started to use broadcast advertising to build community awareness and reputation out of frustration with persistent stereotyping and ignorance among global audiences. I am not referring here to tourism or investment promotion campaigns that aim at selling a specific product to a target market, which is legitimate. What I am weary of are the paid media campaigns, often referred to as nation or city branding campaigns, that try to convince international audiences what wonderful communities exist "out there" and that the clichés and ignorance are inappropriate. The standard content of such commercials consists of aerial shots of landscape and transport or logistics infrastructure, some well-known tourist attractions, men and women in white coats with test tubes in a lab, an operational factory, some art and heritage, a business meeting or conference, students, tourists downtown or on the beach, beautiful nature and nightlife. In other words, the intention is to show all the wonderful things most communities have to offer. The question is whether this has any effect.

Taking into account the above filters that new information needs to penetrate, I seriously doubt that, if the goal is to improve the overall image, mass media advertising campaigns are effective for community reputation building. I argue this for three reasons.

1. First, with online and digital television, pop-up blockers and other tools it is becoming easier and easier for audiences to limit their exposure to broadcast advertising anyway. In addition, the typical networks on which these commercials are aired are the likes of CNN and BBC World. Such channels are particularly popular among travellers who hardly need to be convinced of the richness of other communities, because they are probably more aware and better informed than most other audiences. So, I would question whether the right people are exposed to the campaign, if the idea is to fight ignorance.

2. Second, how likely is it that people will be paying attention? Most viewers or listeners will question the relevance of a random message about the wonders of some other community somewhere else on the planet. Documentaries, travel shows, or targeted tourism or investment promotion commercials are legitimate because they are relevant to a (self-selected) audience that is in the market for what is on offer. But a random commercial bragging about a long list of achievements, attractions and attributes of some other place and people is hardly relevant to a relatively random audience. What is more, many campaigns are very similar in content, as communities feel that they have to push the idea that they are also serious players in the global system. Lots of communities are projecting ideas of openness, diversity, dynamism, innovation and creativity. Of course, the paradox is that globalisation has resulted in a level playing field, which is precisely the reason why communities need to become more imaginative in order to stand out. Instead, what they do is copy and paste the same message as many other communities. Why would anybody still pay attention?

3. Third, comprehension can also be a barrier as what is communicated is often at odds with the clichés and stereotypical images that ignorant foreign publics have in mind (as explained in Section 5.1). Even if community image campaigns are not ignored, they are barely understood as they contradict existing beliefs. In other words, they do not resonate with the audience. The Northern Belgian Dutch-speaking region of Flanders, known for its medieval cobbled streets and abbey beer; the Canadian province of Nova Scotia which is famous for its whales, lobster, tides and shipwrecks; or Kazakhstan, known for its steppe, nomads and horses; all have been relatively unsuccessful in the past with their strategies to position themselves globally as modern, dynamic and diverse. The problem is that the new claims almost completely contradict existing beliefs among most audiences that have had no prior interaction with the communities concerned.

Acceptance is more likely to occur when claims are made convincingly and by expressing an understanding of the audience's preconceived ideas. Wales, in the United Kingdom, has aired some clever tourism commercials, presenting itself as a region with outstandingly bad mobile reception and muddy mountain bike trails for people who really want to get away. The reason this resonates with audiences is that it puts existing beliefs about Wales as a remote and wet place into a different perspective, yet in a way that is easy to understand and accept (i.e. not contradicting existing associations completely).

5.3 How we assess our reputation

The only way to assess the extent to which communities are admired internationally is to survey human beings around the world. What we aim to understand is each respondent's level of awareness, his or her set of perceptions (image) and attitude towards our community. What is reported is reputation (the aggregate). There are many research and consultancy agencies that provide free or syndicated research reports that aim to provide insight into the reputations of cities and countries. I would argue that the freely available reputation rankings are to be read with some caution. Surveying large numbers of citizens in a wide range of countries (which is what needs to be done) is an expensive business and hence for any organisation to offer image research for free seems counterintuitive and one might question the quality of the data on which such rankings are based.

With syndicated research, international research companies utilise their global reach and national opinion poll panels in countries in which they have a presence or partnership to conduct large-scale representative sample research in order to produce relatively standardised reports that can be sold to multiple clients. The Anholt-GfK Roper Nation Brands Index™ (NBI) and City Brands Index™ (CBI) research programmes are examples of this. They survey over 20,000 respondents in over twenty panel countries to measure the reputation of 50 target countries and cities. The NBI and CBI have their flaws, as I will explain later, but they are serious pieces of market research measuring what it says on the tin – reputation. The freely available reputation indexes often make use of freely available data such as online search and social media behaviour data or community asset listings (none of which really equate to image data) or they limit themselves to small samples or biased samples. They have their uses, but only if interpreted with caution. I would argue that it is better for communities to spend some money on participating in syndicated studies and be able to influence research methods and obtain transparency.

The reason why reputation measurement is rather tricky is because of the survey method. Measuring awareness is fairly straightforward and well established. It can easily be done in large-scale surveys with standardised questions and response scales like: 'which countries/cities can you name on the continent of X?' (unaided name awareness); 'have you heard of or are you familiar with country/city X?': 'never heard of' to 'very familiar' (aided name recognition); 'have you ever visited country/city X?' (prominence).

To measure image is trickier as it is hard to standardise the set of associations that determines the image of all communities. For comparability and efficiency in large-scale surveying one would prefer to apply quantitative data collection techniques with standardised questionnaires that consist of mostly closed questions with limited response categories. That allows for rapid data collection and statistical analysis. However, as explained above, perceptions vary between cultural and social groups and many image associations are uniquely linked to a particular community or set of communities. This implies that in order to get a complete picture of what people around the world think of a community, qualitative research tools, like word association, sentence completion or story-telling techniques are needed.

Think of the example above (Section 5.1) of story-telling techniques being used to elicit people's pre-visit image of the city of Dubai. Most schemata that respondents report include common types of perceptual attributes that apply to many places and are included in standardised image research. These include: cultural distance, climate, infrastructure, landscape (desert), activities (shopping) and service levels (luxury). However, many respondents also commented on the position of women in Muslim society, a perception issue among predominantly Western audiences in relation to communities in the Middle East. Even though this association can have a significant impact on Western attitudes towards these communities, it is unlikely that standardised questionnaires will incorporate this kind of image association. It really is a trade-off between measurement validity (are we measuring what we intended to and are we getting a complete picture?) and reliability (test-retest reliability, is it representative of the population?). Considering the variation in communities and perspectives, the list of potentially relevant image associations is endless and hence difficult to encompass in a fully representative standardised global survey.

To solve this conundrum, what some reputation indexes actually do is to measure the attitudinal consequences of image. Surveys focus on questions such as: will you travel there, invest there, buy from there, hire people from there, have friends from there, consume culture from there or trust the government there? This is highly relevant from the perspective of reputation, but the downside is that changes in reputation can sometimes be hard to interpret if there is no data on the changing underlying image associations that have caused the shift in attitude. This is the case for the NBI and CBI as well as other indexes. Also, because the NBI and CBI include measurements among audiences that vary on a wide scale of familiar to unfamiliar, it is unclear whether average scores are caused by lack of awareness or, indeed, a weak image and indifferent or negative attitude. Top positions in the index are usually taken by communities that are well known and admired. At the bottom we find those that are infamous and disliked. However, for countries/cities that are somewhere in between, it is not immediately clear whether the challenge is to raise awareness or to strengthen the image. This can be gauged, though, by looking at the specific name awareness and familiarity questions asked in most surveys. So, even though the advantage of the NBI and CBI is that they truly measure international reputation (i.e. what is in the minds of global audiences), they have their disadvantage in the lack of qualitative data.

Nevertheless, because of its standardisation, consistency and longitudinality, the NBI produces interesting insights. First of all, it shows that reputations are rather stable. This can be seen in Figure 2, which depicts the annual ranking in the Anholt-GfK Roper Nation Brands Index™ (NBI) for five countries that hosted mega-events between 2008 and 2016. It shows that rankings do not change very much and even mega-events have little impact. In fact, the impact can even be somewhat negative, such as in the case of South Africa and Brazil, where community problems seem to have been magnified under the powerful planetary telescope of the global media that mega-events attract. In 2014, while Brazil's reputation declined slightly while organising the FIFA World Cup, Germany gained, partly by winning the competition (which might raise the question whether it is better to invest in an imaginative domestic sports programme that supports athletes than to host games). The London Olympics did not do much for the reputation of the UK, but how could it, if the country was already consistently number three in the index, with strong contenders Germany and the United States ahead of it? As Simon Anholt has argued, the British put on a good show, as expected, representing popular culture and British humour, which is already admired. They paid the rent on their reputation, which is built slowly and needs maintenance, but can usually not be expected to shoot up. The exception in Figure 2 is China, which made a concerted effort to showcase its technological prowess and development. As a result, the attitudes towards Chinese exports and the sophistication of the Chinese people significantly improved. However, as indicated, such success is uncommon and requires concerted and imaginative efforts.

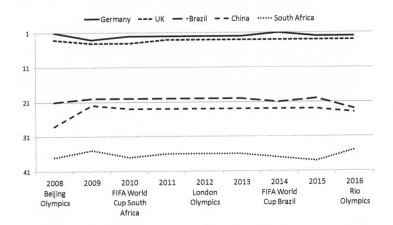

Figure 2: The impact of mega-events on country reputation based on NBI rank (out of 50)

Table 7 shows that indeed, as argued, perceptions are influenced by the cultural and social background of the perceiver, besides personal and psychological characteristics. Table 7 shows the category rankings of not-to-be-named Asian country X on the six image dimensions of the NBI (i.e. Simon Anholt's Nation Brand Hexagon) in the twenty panel countries in which measurement took place in 2016. It is clear that country X's reputation is generally rather weak, with slightly better perceptions on governance and the people of country X.

Table 7: Country X's Index Rank (out of 50) per NBI Hexagon Dimension per panel country (2016)

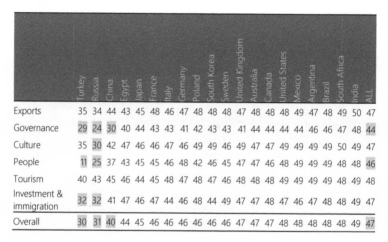

	Turkey	Russia	China	Egypt	Japan	France	Italy	Germany	Poland	South Korea	Sweden	United Kingdom	Australia	Canada	United States	Mexico	Argentina	Brazil	South Africa	India	ALL
Exports	35	34	44	43	45	48	46	47	48	48	48	47	48	48	48	49	47	48	49	50	47
Governance	29	24	30	40	44	43	43	41	42	43	43	41	44	44	44	44	46	46	47	48	44
Culture	35	30	42	47	46	46	47	46	49	49	46	49	47	47	49	49	49	49	50	49	47
People	11	25	37	43	45	45	46	48	42	46	45	47	47	46	48	49	49	49	48	48	46
Tourism	40	43	45	46	44	45	48	47	48	47	46	48	48	48	49	49	49	49	48	49	48
Investment & immigration	32	32	41	47	46	47	44	46	48	44	49	47	47	48	47	46	47	48	48	49	47
Overall	30	31	40	44	45	46	46	46	46	46	46	47	47	47	48	48	48	48	48	49	47

However, the reputation of country X in China is generally somewhat stronger than in most other countries and it is particularly well regarded by the Russians and Turks, who seem to feel more allied to the people of country X and their government. This is most likely to do with proximity and historical ties, confirming that an overall ranking is one thing, but even though it seems quite stable over time, there is real value in looking at the detail, meaning specific image association and cultural variations among audiences. For one thing, familiarity can influence attitude. This is shown in Figure 3, which plots relative familiarity against favourability for a country in the Middle East as measured in panel countries. In the overall ranking, this country ranks somewhere in the fourth quadrant, so it doesn't score particularly well globally. However, this seems to be more of an awareness problem than an attitude problem as respondents in survey panels that are more familiar with this country perceive it more favourably than respondents that are not. This is not always the case. Figure 4 shows the same plot of familiarity versus favourability for a country in Africa that consistently ranks at the bottom of the NBI. In that case it is a problem of both awareness and negative attitude as panels with relatively higher familiarity still seem to dislike this country.

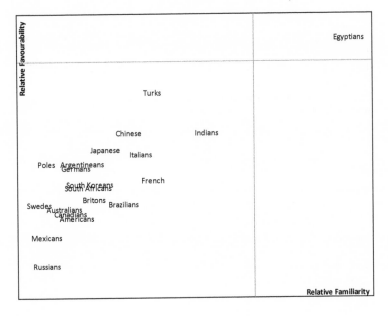

Figure 3: Relative familiarity versus favourability for a country in the Middle East as measured in panel countries

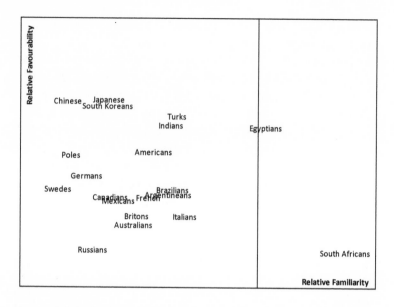

Figure 4: Relative familiarity versus favourability for a country in Africa as measured in panel countries

Chapter 6
What they convey: Imaged communities

Admiration is attained by those communities that set the news and broadcasting agenda and create content that audiences share in social media.

People tend to hold on to their image of the world and its communities; they do not like to change their fundamental beliefs as these are comforting ways of reducing complexity. As a result, community reputations are generally conservative, static and based on influential stereotypes. To change this is a colossal task and requires a continuous and persistent flow of imaginative identity-reinforcing initiatives that stack up to a wall of evidence that a particular community does not deserve to be reduced to the sort of stereotypes and clichés it is being labelled with. This chapter will show that such a task requires much more than communication, particularly in today's hyper-mobile and hyper-connected world. Classic strategic communication is at an end as we now live in the age of what I would refer to as "action communication", in the sense that reputations are built by what you do and not by what you say about yourself. Actions speak much louder than words.

6.1 What they absorb

The reason why actions speak louder than words is, of course, the fact that the most important source of information on which people base their perceptions and opinions is their own experience. "Seeing is believing" is an ancient idiom, but it is still highly relevant today. Travellers visiting a community for the first time dramatically change their mind about the place. The student studying abroad or the expat worker living overseas becomes a different person. The food that we eat and the products that we buy from somewhere impact our assumptions about other communities. Most importantly, meeting people from other cultures impacts radically who we are and how we see the world. Experiences are by far the most important vehicle through which we can create understanding. They allow us to "see in high resolution" – in more detail, appreciating the diversity and complexity. Hence the success of cultural and educational exchange programmes. By 2014 the European Union's Erasmus study programme was responsible for one million transnational babies, as more than a quarter of those who participate in the programme meet their long-term partner while studying abroad.[17] It is hard to imagine a more effective way of facilitating European integration and inter-community understanding.

The second most important information vehicle for people to form perceptions about other communities is word of mouth. When lacking personal experiences, people tend to rely to a large extent on their peers – people like themselves. Favourite topics for conversations at parties and get-togethers are people's travels and cultural experiences. They love to share stories about their last overseas trip or that new exotic cuisine that they discovered. This has always been the case, but, of course, with the internet and social media, the impact of this has gone through the roof. It is not surprising that travel is one of the most important categories of online activity and the review systems for places and locations have taken the world by storm. As early as 2002, years before the launch of Facebook, Twitter or Instagram, John Riedl and Joseph Konstan predicted the future significance of "word of mouse"[18] and they were clearly right, as social media has become a major information vehicle for many.

The third most important information vehicle for people to form perceptions about other communities, are the autonomous broadcast/mainstream news media. Because of their high credibility and market penetration, these may be the only information vehicles capable of rapidly creating a dramatic change to a community's image. One of the reasons for this may be that news does not age well and major events often receive massive attention over a relatively short period of time. However, without reinforcement, in time, images are likely to revert back to what they were before. This can either be positive or negative, but whatever the case, one would expect that communities would want to influence this process. That's why "stealth vehicles" are becoming increasingly important.

Stealth operations make use of broadcasting media and popular culture to influence perceptions without mentioning a clearly identified sponsor. In that way they are different from advertising; less conspicuous and invasive. Promising developments in the production of vicarious experiences through virtual reality, immersive media and gaming can also be exploited in this way. The potential of this has been acknowledged for years. For instance, as a result of the success of the movie *Troy*, starring Brad Pitt, the western Turkish city of Çanakkale, the location of ancient Troy, had seen a 73 per cent increase in visitor numbers. This number increased further when the Trojan horse used in the film was re-used as a visitor attraction. In New Zealand, tourism is said to have increased as a result of its exposure as the backdrop for the movie trilogy *The Lord of the Rings*. Over seven per cent of visitors to New Zealand claimed to be influenced by the movies. Hawaii's exposure in television shows (*North Shore*, *Hawaii* and *Lost*) and movies

(*American Idol*) has helped boost visitor numbers and *Game of Thrones* has overwhelmed Dubrovnik. These are processes that communities can influence or take advantage of. In fact, Hawaii had to actively lobby and enter a competition with other locations in an effort to get producers to film on the island.[19] The nature of many formerly autonomous agents has therefore changed to become stealth vehicles.

Finally, paid advertising has proven to be the least effective way in which communities can attempt to shed stereotypes and clichés. With media consumption people have become experienced in separating paid messages, perceived as unreliable, from autonomous reporting or word of mouth, regardless of the "fake news" rhetoric. Many people even aim to avoid advertising by using digital television, pop-up blockers and the do-not-call registry. This has significantly reduced the effectiveness and efficiency of advertising, which should therefore be deployed with caution. In fact, in the battle against clichés and stereotypes, advertising may even be counter-productive, as audiences do not like to be told that they are wrong. Alternatively, they are likely to evaluate messages as incomprehensible, implausible or even confirmatory (for example, the reaction may be: 'if this is what they have to pay advertising agencies for, the reality must be even worse than we thought').

6.2 What they share

What changes people's minds are experiences – their own or those of others that are shared. Imaginative identity-reinforcing initiatives create the kind of experiences and pieces of content that generate engagement. With social media, the distinction between community development and communication becomes increasingly blurred anyway. With developments such as Google Maps/Earth-based information delivery, augmented reality, location-based services and information provision, and peer-to-peer engagement and reviews, communication depends on action. Cooperation between stakeholders and information vehicles is essential for this. The trick is to activate all information vehicles and the only way to do this is to create shareable experiences through imaginative action.

This is also the way to break through the agenda setting and framing deployed by mainstream media, which are just as likely to stick to clichés and stereotypes. Agenda-setting theory contends that the mass media have the ability to influence the prominence of topics on the public agenda and hence to sway public opinion (whether or not through a reciprocal process of agenda building and setting with politicians and PR). Media framing, on the other hand, is concerned with the way in which issues are reported (with moral, causal and emotional judgements). In other words, agenda setting aims to determine what people should *think about* (attention and awareness), while framing influences what people *think* (comprehension and image). Consider, for instance, how, generally, countries and cities in Africa are consistently framed as basket cases, war-torn communities governed by corrupt elites exploiting resources on the back of poor and starving populations. African communities consistently lag behind in reputation building having to correct these negative clichés and stereotypes.

Agenda setting and framing not only influence what people think about and how they think, but also what people think that others are thinking about and how they think. This suggests that it also influences social media behaviour as people are more likely to like and share posts that they think others will find interesting or funny. Hence, even though social media, being demand driven rather than pushing, reduce the effect of agenda setting and framing, mainstream media still appear to influence what is being covered and how, even on social media. This got everyone talking about Donald Trump during the 2016 US presidential elections. Whether he was covered as a serious candidate or a laughing stock was irrelevant. He was at the forefront of the debate, no matter how strong his opponents and how serious their policy proposals compared to his.

However, in most countries politics is losing public interest and politicians are dealing with a disengaged electorate. Travel, culture and people, on the other hand, are areas of high interest that audiences love to share stories about. Personal experiences, in particular, result in bragging rights online. This is a powerful mechanism through which communities can aim to influence their reputations and even reverse the agenda-setting mechanism with audiences determining the public agenda. An example of a community that imaginatively created its own story across various media vehicles was Queensland.

Tourism Queensland's Best Job in the World campaign is a good example of action communication. It won the prestigious Cannes Lions PR Award and generated tremendous audience engagement with a limited budget. Instead of spending large sums on paid mass media advertising, Tourism Queensland posted classified ads all over the world offering what they called the best job in the world: a position as island caretaker with a $8,800 a month salary and a rent-free three-bedroomed villa with plunge pool.

On day one of the campaign www.islandreefjob.com received four million hits an hour (more hits in the UK than google.com). After the six-week application process the website had received almost 3.5 million unique visitors and almost 35,000 video applications had been posted. This generated 6,000 news stories worldwide and media coverage worth an estimated US$80 million. The social media engagement generated by the initiative (based on real action-based content) was the key to its success. People shared the story and the engagement experiences of applicants, because it exploited the dream of a better life that we all have. This resulted in a shockwave of word of mouth and mouse through social media, which was then picked up by news agencies and in mainstream media programming, resulting in media integration across channels.

The Tourism Queensland campaign shows what imaginative initiatives can do in the age of the social web. Traditional advertising and spin will no longer win the hearts and minds of a global audience. Creative use of technologies will allow communities to co-create identities, experiences and imaginaries. Involvement of stakeholders, public and private actors and civil society, as well as the global audience of vocal individuals who take part in the conversation, is key. On the other hand, relying totally on the dynamics of the social web will also be risky. As Keen (2007)[20] notes, the cult of the amateur might kill our culture and assault our economy, so, as the Queensland case illustrates, initiation, guidance and readjustment by public agencies is still needed. Communities should provide strategic positioning, based on identity, but in a transparent, accessible and imaginative manner which looks for dialogue and engagement, based on real action and substance. This would allow the activation of all information vehicles.

6.3 How we assess our exposure

Media monitoring is well established through the method of content analysis. There are many different types of content analysis, ranging from simple frequency counts – increasingly done by computers, based on media databases – to complicated assessments of arguments and media frames. Several organisations provide such analyses for cities, regions and countries. Media Tenor conducts studies that are based on the analysis of the content of TV news in eleven media markets by trained coders of the Zürich-based research institute Media Tenor International. Schatz and Kolmer of Media Tenor[21] report on a study of the visibility of eleven countries in the international media, how the visibility changes over time, and based on what issues. Cromwell of East West

Communications[22] reports on the 'East West Nation Brand
Perception Indexes that rank 200 nations (that is, the 192 member
states of the United Nations, as well as eight major territories, such
as Hong Kong) in quarterly and annual listings based on scores
they achieve derived from the tone of news coverage received in a
given period. Coverage of these nations is analysed in several
dozen major international publications by algorithms that assess
tone [or sentiment] in text through the grammatical association of
words and phrases with proper nouns. For most countries, there is
considerable fluctuation in scores from quarter to quarter, and
national events, and reporting on those events, can be correlated
with scores, enabling countries to get a good sense of what in their
news is driving perceptions up, and what down.'

However, both these tools rely on major news channels only. An
alternative is to use online monitoring tools. Radian6, for instance,
provides content and sentiment analysis based on both mainstream
and social media. It scans the full Twitter Firehose of public tweets;
over half a billion posts scoured from more than 1 billion social
media sources every day (growing at the rate of five million new
sources every week); millions of blog sites; hundreds of thousands
of top online news sites including CNN, BBC, *New York Times*, and
Huffington Post; over 450 video- and image-sharing sites including
YouTube, Vimeo and Flickr; nearly one million forums and
discussions boards; and LinkedIn Open Groups in over 26
languages. The main metrics used here are number of postings and
sentiment score. Although the former is a straightforward
quantitative count, the latter requires a more complex automated
process of assessing whether the posts, and in particular their
qualitative content, are positive, neutral or negative in sentiment.
Automated sentiment analysis is based on the idea that there is a
conceptual connection between words that are grammatically
linked (as described in the East West Communications quote
above). Sentiment towards a target term within a sentence is
calculated by measuring the number of co-occurrences of the
target term and a pre-defined list of sentiment words known to

have positive or negative sentiment. This type of analysis relies on the work of linguists and is already used to a large extent in natural language processing. However, because sentiment words are not necessarily always used, particularly in short postings such as on microblogs (e.g. Twitter), or in comments on social media in general, many postings are categorised as neutral. Also, whether manual or automated, sentiment analysis is always subjective and does not take into account aspects such as sarcasm, irony or personal interpretations by an individual reader (what is negative for one person can be positive for someone else). Nevertheless, large changes in the proportions of positively versus negatively categorised postings can provide an indication of general changes in sentiment among the social media buzz.

As an example, to illustrate the kind of analyses that media monitoring produces, a search was conducted on the Radian6 platform for postings that included mention of Dubai, Abu Dhabi, Bahrain (and/or Manama) or Qatar (and/or Doha). It is obvious that Bahrain and Qatar were included as nations and/or their capitals, while Abu Dhabi and Dubai are both Emirates and corresponding cities with the same name as part of the federation of United Arab Emirates. However, it was considered that at a community level this is not an issue as indeed Abu Dhabi and Dubai seem to be positioned as separate competing communities while the country does not seem (to want to) boast a strong awareness or reputation as a whole (for instance, there is no national or federal tourism promotion board).

The daily number of postings in mainstream versus all media channels for the three-year period 30 June 2008 to 30 June 2011 is depicted in Figures 5 and 6.

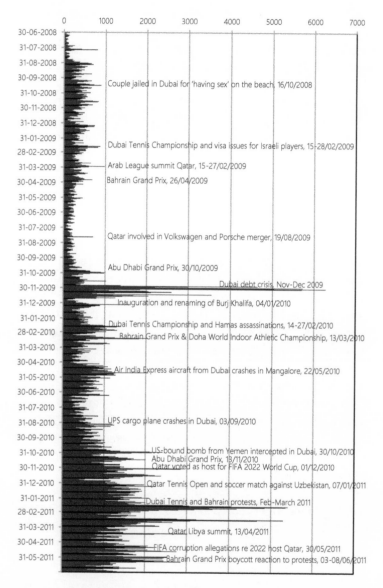

Figure 5: The number of posts on news media websites linked to events in Dubai, Abu Dhabi, Bahrain (and/or Manama) or Qatar (and/or Doha) between June 2008 and June 2011. Source: author's interpretation of Radian6 data.

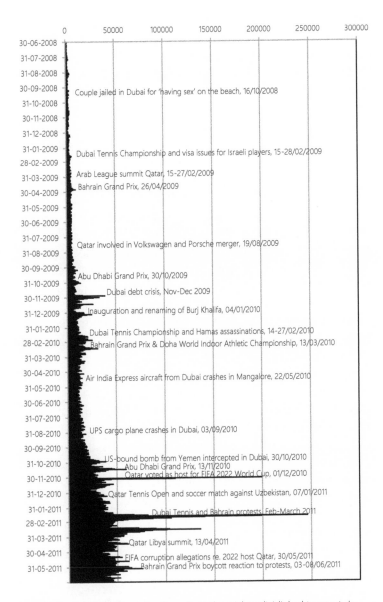

Figure 6: The number of posts in all media (incl. social media) linked to events in Dubai, Abu Dhabi, Bahrain (and/or Manama) or Qatar (and/or Doha) between June 2008 and June 2011. Source: author's interpretation of Radian6 data.

Generally Dubai generates most of the buzz, remaining in "calm waters" up to November 2009, after which there is a period of increased attention with the Dubai debt crisis, the inauguration of the Burj Dubai (and its simultaneous renaming to Burj Khalifa) on 4 January 2010, as well as the Dubai Tennis Championship and simultaneous Hamas assassinations in Dubai during February 2010. However, since then, the competition has succeeded in occasionally attracting a significant buzz, for instance with the Abu Dhabi and Bahrain Grand Prix. In fact, it seems that the whole region has been attracting more attention since the beginning of 2010, although this might also be a reflection of increased use of social media. Two events, however, had a dramatic impact on global attention. First, the selection of Qatar by FIFA to host the 2022 World Cup generated off-scale postings totalling 178,116 in all social media, including "only" 2,433 postings on news media websites. Second, the Bahrain protests as part of the Arab Spring generated a tremendous amount of buzz over an extended period: the highest number of posts on a single day was off the scale both in news media and social media postings, totalling 4,334 and an astonishing 214,631 respectively.

What is also interesting is the swing in sentiment that events can cause. Figure 7 shows that over extended periods, in this case the second quarter (1 April–30 June) of 2009, 2010 and 2011, which are relatively stable periods without many major events, the sentiment is steady with, as expected considering its dominance in social media, relatively lots of positive attention for Dubai, but also some negative (note that the majority of neutral postings is not included in these graphs for legibility and that sentiment analysis is conducted on news media postings only as the amount of data would otherwise overload the system; it is assumed that news media sentiment is similarly reflected in social media sentiment). In the second quarter of 2010 the buzz on Dubai is more balanced with positive as well as negative, probably as a result of the Dubai debt crisis. The increase in negative buzz on Bahrain as a result of opposition protests in the second quarter of 2011 is also clearly identifiable.

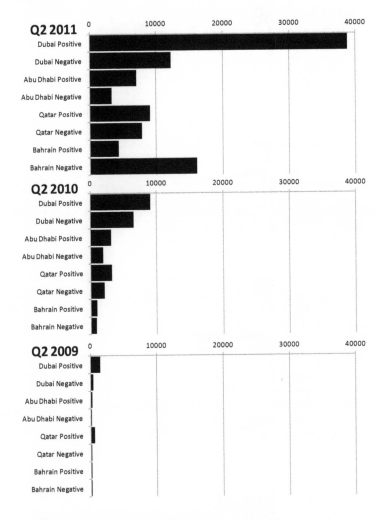

Figure 7: Examples of sentiment in number of posts in mainstream news media websites in second quarter 2009, 2010 and 2011 (excluding neutral postings). Source: Provided by Radian6 Analysis Dashboard™ July 2011.

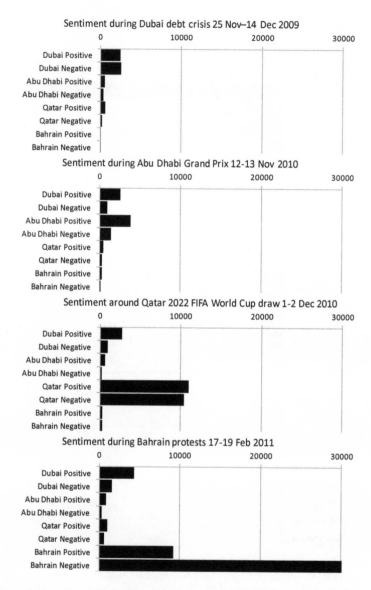

Figure 8: Examples of sentiment in all media during major news events (excluding neutral postings). Source: Provided by Radian6 Analysis Dashboard™ July 2011.

However, Figure 8 shows what dramatic impact particular events can have on sentiment in all social media over a shorter period of time. During the Dubai debt crisis in November to December 2009 the generally positive buzz on Dubai was balanced out with lots of negative coverage. The Abu Dhabi Grand Prix warrants short-term dominance with positive coverage as did the selection of Qatar to host the World Cup in 2022, even though there were some negative sentiments about this as well. Lastly, buzz in the region was suddenly dominated in the second quarter of 2011 with negative sentiment as a result of the Bahrain protests.

What is also notable in Figures 5 and 6 is that some events gain news media attention without much social media buzz, such as the April 2011 Doha summit on Libya or the Arab League summits, while other events generate relatively more social media buzz as opposed to mainstream media attention, for example, the Bahrain protests or sports (related) events. Note that indoor athletics and Formula One racing get similar coverage in the news media, but the latter generates much more buzz in the social media.

It is interesting to see in the above analysis what dramatic effect certain events can have on social media buzz and how important social media have become. Some types of events seem to be more effective in attracting social media coverage than others and it would therefore be of particular interest to conduct future research on how this impacts public opinion and reputation. Similarly, some events have longevity while others have a short term hype effect. Again, it would be interesting to study which type of buzz has most impact. On the one hand repetition of a message increases impact, but on the other hand, a short-lived tsunami of buzz similar to the attention that Qatar has attracted as a result of the World Cup 2022 vote will guarantee that most individuals on the planet will have heard about such an achievement and might firmly establish a place on the map (including people's mind-map). Again, this assumption would warrant corroboration in future research.

The most important conclusion that should be drawn from the above analysis is that media coverage is highly volatile. While community identity and reputation can literally take generations to change significantly, media coverage is highly event driven. So it is quite obvious that reputation management is much more than a communications challenge.

Chapter 7
What they experience: Community imagineering

Communities can engineer imaginative experiences to appeal to audiences' dreams; the stuff that people talk about.

The reason why communities need to come up with imaginative projects, policies, investments or events is because they allow publics to engage in captivating experiences, in situ, but also virtually, online, in virtual reality or in gaming. In community imagineering these 'are core elements in building physical manifestations of the [community's] (desired) global qualities by infusing festivals, sporting events, buildings, parks, squares, roads, even whole neighbourhoods, with symbolic meaning'.[23] Community imagineering is an 'attempt to connect to a global imaginary, while simultaneously appropriating the "cultural" realm as a means of maintaining a sense of unique identity'.[24] This creation of experience environments was invented by Walt Disney Studios, who define imagineering as 'combining imagination with engineering to create the reality of dreams' in their theme parks.[25]

The appeal of community engagement – experience – is derived from the interfacing between host and guest, the outcome of which can have an impact on reputation. Cultural differences are likely to complicate matters. Of course, continued international engagement will alleviate this problem through learning. Therefore, it is expected that familiarity with a certain place and the level of involvement of the "visitor" with it, will influence the perceived image. The information acquired through personal experience forms the primary image, which may differ from the secondary image which was examined in the chapter above. Indeed post-visit image tends to be more realistic, complex and different from the pre-visit images that are based on secondary sources of information. However, with the growth of social media, the extensive sharing of personal experiences obviously creates a whole new dynamic.

7.1 How they experience

Utilitarian community functions such as transport, security or financial systems are obviously important, but they seem to have a limited positive impact on reputation. Among a general global audience very few communities are famous for their efficient border systems, intermodal transport connections or insurance services. Of course, on a macro level, the extent to which communities are properly organised or not influences reputations, but very rarely does this involve specificities.

What does make a difference is the way in which audiences experience community spirit. Very specific icons, celebrities, art works, historical events or productions of popular culture are ingrained in people's minds. Community leaders should be paying much more attention to finding imaginative ways in which these can facilitate real and virtual experiences of community identity. Policy makers too often focus on utilitarian functions. That is understandable because such functions are crucial elements that allow communities to prosper and they are easily made accountable in quantifiable terms. Also, when things go wrong, reputations are easily damaged in the short term if they are dealing with uncontrollable incidents. Sometimes there can even be long-term damage in case of repetition and incompetence. Yet, when things go well, success in these functional areas doesn't usually result in specific reputational value, particularly as globalisation has created a level playing field. One could say that utilitarian functions are hygiene factors – when delivered according to expectation they are taken for granted, but absence leads to dissatisfaction.

When people engage with other communities, be it in person or online, what they will often remember are the unique experiences of local character, *couleur locale* or *genius loci*. Rich and distinctive experiences tend to stick. Rich experiences are, of course, multisensory. Our lives and memories are very much focused on language and visuals. Yet, sensory experiences of certain uncommon aromas or flavours that we find hard to reproduce from memory can sometimes throw us back immediately to a certain time and/or place when re-encountered. In my research about the pre-visit perceptions of places, respondents refer to the smell of spices in oriental souks or the taste of specific local dishes. Multisensory encounters are more memorable, because more sensory stimuli will activate the schemata.

The sensory impressions interact with what is stored in memory – cognitive processes linking perceptual observations to existing concepts, contexts and meanings, including processes of imagination, creating and re-creating fantasies and providing "meaning". Based on stereotypes, clichés and preconceived ideas, people have expectations that they hope to fulfil and enrich when they engage in unfamiliar activities. This potentially generates emotional responses, such as joy, fear, expectancy, sadness or surprise, which, again, make experiences more memorable.

Active involvement and participation, unlike passive gazing, also enhances memorability, particularly if social interactions are included. Elements of competition, gaming, mental stimulation, physical activity, conversation with locals and others, the sharing of food, song or dance, will leave lasting impressions and create more remarkable encounters.

Consider, for instance, the way in which most communities deal with mega-events. Most of the time organisers of mega-events, such as Olympic Games or football world championships, put most of their efforts into making sure the logistics, coverage and infrastructure run smoothly. Communities think that if they are capable of organising a great event, the world will love them. The opposite is true; if an event becomes a disaster, reputations might be damaged, but on the other hand, a smoothly running event is not remarkable at all, it is expected and a minimal requirement. The relevant question that organisers should ask themselves is how they can use the event to get people to experience the community in imaginative ways. One successful example of this was the 2006 football World Cup in Germany. Apart from running a very well organised event (as one would expect from the Germans), the country was able to turn around the perception of "the German" as being unfriendly, unwelcoming and formal. By creating engaging experiences in the form of fan zones (in Germany and participating countries), friendly and engaging international security forces (from participating countries) at the stadiums, and joined-up arts and cultural programmes, the Germans were able to surprise visitors and the press by contradicting stereotypes, generating emotional responses and changing international perceptions.

7.2 How they enjoy (flow)

Experiences that are '*autotelic*, or rewarding in and of itself' have been termed states of "flow" or "optimal experience" by Csikszentmihalyi. The flow experience is characterised by several dimensions, particularly a balance between challenge and skills. When the demands are too high, it results in a feeling of anxiety. When the demands are too low, the person might get bored. Other common characteristics of flow experiences include focused concentration and a distorted sense of time. People in flow commonly have no attention left to think of anything else. Although in flow experiences clear goals, and quick and unambiguous feedback on performance, are needed, the goals are often just an excuse to make the experience possible. The adventurer who aims to visit that distant community does not travel to reach the destination; he aims to visit the community in order to experience adventure. Gamers do not want to progress through the next level and the next in order to finish the game; they want to challenge their skills.

There are some famous examples of communities that have created uniquely local flow experiences for audiences to enjoy. In the Pamplona Bull Run men sprint in front of a small herd of bulls through the streets of Pamplona in an attempt to make it safely to the bullring without being overtaken or hurt. The Indian Holi Colour Run celebrates the Hindu Holi spring festival with a five-kilometre run, in which participants are doused with colourful powder at kilometre checkpoints. Less famous are the increasingly popular local city games that integrate on- and offline and gaming with local storytelling.

Flow experiences are characterised by clear goals and immediate, accurate and unambiguous feedback on performance. Imaginative and memorable experiences are often the ones that are uncommon, surprising, emotional, engaging and intense (multisensory). This takes people out of their comfort zone in an effort to challenge them and get their attention. However, this could also be distressing and hence it is essential to inform audiences of what is expected and to provide information on what is happening during events. For instance, at the Pamplona Bull Run participants are informed that the total distance covered is 875 metres and that it takes two to three minutes for the bulls to traverse the track at an average speed of 24 kilometres an hour. During the run rockets are fired into the air. A first rocket is set off at 8 a.m. to alert the runners that the corral gate is open. A second rocket signals that all six bulls have been released. The third and fourth rockets are signals that the whole herd has entered the bullring and its corral respectively, marking the end of the event.

The optimal experience is achieved when people are challenged to the extent that they can match their skills, balancing between boredom and anxiety. It's always a challenge when outsiders engage with unfamiliar communities, particularly when there is cultural distance involved. Hence, opportunities for flow are intrinsic. In the Pamplona Bull Run, a Spanish athlete might get bored; a foreign athlete probably not so much. However, someone who is unfit to run might become anxious rather quickly as the bulls approach. Allowing for variation in levels of engagement and effort is therefore usually a good idea when designing community experiences.

One knows that a state of flow is achieved when action and awareness are merged. People start to completely ignore distractions as they concentrate entirely on the activity. Even self-consciousness disappears and failure is not a consideration. In the Pamplona Bull Run people do actually get hurt, but still thousands participate thinking that failure is not an option, they are fully concentrated on their fellow runners and where the bulls are. Focused concentration leads to a distorted sense of time: hours seem to pass by in minutes, and occasionally a few seconds stretch out into what seems to be an eternity.

Csikszentmihalyi argues that the concept of flow is always relevant when aiming for meaningful human experiences. Many people engage with other communities in order to escape from boredom and anxiety and to experience a heightened state of being. But it is a balancing act. The examples above illustrate that developing community engagement is an intricate business – specifically, whom to challenge up to what level? The demands on people's skills while engaging with new communities will be above average for most individuals in comparison to their everyday lives.

This is probably true for most interactions with unfamiliar communities, from people on package tours or routine business travellers to adventure travellers, migrant workers or international students, as demands are assessed relative to the individual's everyday life, and different types of community experience probably attract different audiences with different domestic backgrounds and hence different skills. Studies show that many travellers report feelings of harmony with the environment, focused concentration, liminality, losing track of time, and the attractiveness of the act of travelling for its own sake. At the same time this implies that visitors are often balancing on a thin line between boredom and anxiety. The latter is often the cause of dissatisfaction: an experience is all too easily ruined if even the smallest thing goes wrong and the demands placed on the visitor exceed their skills. What really makes a difference, though, is information provision. It is not the disruptions or unexpected situations, but not knowing what is going on and what to expect (goals and feedback) that people find most frustrating. Hence, imaginative communities should not just be thinking about product (infrastructures, projects, icons, stage settings), but just as much about process and how participants co-create the experience.

7.3 How we enchant

Meaningful experiences are created in experience environments by experience networks. Multiple public, private and civil society actors collaborate in a network in order to create a community offering that allows audiences to co-create their own personalised experiences. Travel experiences are typical in that they require transport, accommodation, catering, and other service and information providers to collaborate, and to align and provide access to their offerings, transparently. If this is done by network members that have a sense of identity and belonging, while understanding the expectations and preconceived perceptions of audiences, imaginative initiatives potentially result in unique experience environments that allow for emotional responses and active involvement – the kind of stuff that people will share in social media. Special events are temporary and hence easier to design and dramatise as experience environments. Because they take place for a limited time, it is easier to rally the experience network behind them and ask members to put extra effort in. Events are therefore effective catalysts for partnerships.

Events have some other advantages as vehicles for imaginative initiatives. Events can easily be value matched: themed, designed and staged so as to reflect a match between the identity of the local community, the imagination of the network actors and the anticipation of the audience. This crucial value-matching perspective often slips between the cracks of the intensive preparation, planning and organisation of mega-events, which is a real shame, as that is the vital ingredient for using the massive media megaphone to one's advantage. A successful event is just that. An enchanting event has the potential to showcase distinctiveness and be meaningful and memorable. By generating (social) media attention it potentially builds reputation.

Events also allow for active resident participation and hence engagement with visitors. During the 2006 World Cup in Germany this was a crucial ingredient of the strategy to change the international reputation of the Germans. A national campaign with the motto 'Germany is rolling out the red carpet' targeted the German population, primarily the media, the tourism sector and other people who would most likely come into contact with foreign visitors, such as airport staff and taxi drivers. The campaign aimed to prepare Germans for their role as hosts of the World Cup and to motivate people to be welcoming, tolerant and respectful.

Austin

Musicians and fans of country, roots rock and blues can easily identify an "Austin sound". It emerged internationally in the late 1960s and early 1970s, when several non-conformist musicians moved to Austin, most notably Willie Nelson. *Austin City Limits*, broadcast since 1974, is the longest-running music series in television history.

Austin, the capital city of the state of Texas, is only the eleventh most populous city in the United States, but because of its musical roots, it has established a global reputation as the live music capital of the world. With around 200 live music venues Austin offers more performances than other US cities known for music like Nashville, New Orleans or Memphis. The city breathes music and offers a unique musical experience. Nevertheless, in the 1980s

Austinites still felt that while the local creative and music communities were as talented as anywhere else on the planet, they were severely limited by lack of exposure outside Austin.

The solution was to create an event that would bring the world to Austin in order for outside audiences to experience the creative power of the city for themselves, as opposed to advertising it. South by Southwest (SXSW) was created. As hoped for, Austin's charm won over the visitors, and SXSW took on a life of its own. Nowadays, the South by Southwest Conference & Festivals celebrates the convergence of the interactive, film and music industries. It is marketed as the premier destination for discovery. The event runs for a full ten days and nights with – in 2018 – a 24-track conference with close to 5,000 speakers; a music festival with over 2,000 showcasing artists and 320 panels, workshops and sessions in over 100 venues and stages; and a film festival with 455 screenings and 145 world premieres. In 2018 approximately 432,500 people participated in the SXSW Conference & Festivals. Most importantly, in 2017 the value of SXSW print, broadcast and online publications coverage totalled US$572.3 million. Austin has become the undisputed and acknowledged annual destination to absorb, be touched by and engage with the creative industries, which is largely thanks to a large number of fruitful local partnerships and thousands of volunteers.

Gaudí's Barcelona or Manrique's Lanzarote

In the nineteenth century, industrial and commercial activities brought tremendous wealth to Barcelona. However, the city's expansion was obstructed by the medieval city walls, within which population density became unbearable. This led to one of the most ambitious nineteenth-century urban expansion projects in Europe. This renewal and prosperity also created a new social class, a bourgeoisie that acquired affluence within a short span of time. These *nouveaux riches* bought social status by spending more money on luxury goods and appearance than the dull nobility, bankers and traditional merchants.

While modernism was spreading across Europe, in Catalonia and Barcelona in particular, it reached great heights in terms of social relevance, vitality and originality, even though it was not supported by any kind of academic platform or state subsidy. Despite the lack of an organising platform, Catalan modernism became the driving force for renewal and modernisation, not just in literature and music, but most importantly, in transforming Barcelona into one gigantic open-air architecture museum as the city expanded. For the young industrial and financial bourgeoisie the new architecture allowed them to buy social status through showpiece residences on Barcelona's new boulevards and shopping high-streets, built to be admired outside the city's old medieval quarters.

Even though modernism was taking root across Europe it acquired a unique political dimension in Barcelona. Industrialisation, social mobility and modernisation coincided with the consolidation of the Catalan nationalist movement against the Spanish state. As a result Catalan modernism grew to be associated with a solid political goal and an expression of Catalan national identity. About 80 architects would transform the outer and new ring around the old town of Barcelona as the medieval walls came down. Antoni Gaudí was undoubtedly the most original, inspirational and eccentric of all of them. Yet, at the same time he had the gift of convincing people to commit to his projects. Famous for his Sagrada Família, Casa Milà and Parc Güell, Gaudí still enchants today's visitors to Barcelona. He has been largely responsible for creating a unique Catalan experience that can only be found there.[26]

The same can be said for the island of Lanzarote (one of the Canary Islands in the Atlantic Ocean) where César Manrique – Spanish painter, sculptor and architect – has had a major impact with projects such as Mirador del Río, Jameos del Agua and Jardín de Cactus, as well as El Diablo restaurant in the Timanfaya National

Park and Hotel Gran Meliá Salinas in Costa Teguise. Manrique's wind sculptures adorned many a roundabout on the island, but on his death these were relocated to the Manrique museum.

Manrique helped the island find a balance between tourism development and conservation. He wanted to make sure that buildings were no higher than four floors and were painted white with window frames painted in blue, green or brown. As a result, even though the island is a tourism hotspot it has been able to maintain some of its unique character, offering unique local experiences.

Van Gogh's Nuenen

Nuenen is a small town outside the Dutch city of Eindhoven, in the south of the country. It is a hinterland that would be insignificant from an international perspective, if it was not for the fact that Nuenen is linked with Eindhoven by a unique cycle path. Of course, the flat Low Countries are famous for cycling, but this cycle path is something else. Artist Daan Roosegaarde, assisted by construction company Heijmans, paved it with fluorescent stones that recharge during the day and emit light at night. Roosegaarde wanted to create a place that would inspire people by linking new technology with locally relevant experiences – a kind of "techno-poetry". The twinkling pattern of light and colour on the asphalt contains fragments of Van Gogh's *The Starry Night*, painted in the south of France. However, Van Gogh lived in Nuenen from 1883 to1885. He painted many of the local landscapes, weavers and peasants, as can be seen in his world-famous masterpiece *The Potato Eaters*.
The 600-metre-long path is part of the Van Gogh Cycle Route which links Van Gogh heritage locations in the region. It creates a unique experience that is captivating and locally relevant. It appeals to people's senses and emotions, linking to fantasies of starry nights and Van Gogh, through active involvement as cyclists and as a social activity to be enjoyed together and shared in social media.

ROBERT GOVERS

Chapter 8
How we rise:
Enlightened
communities

Admired communities operate in the landscape of culture and social engagement, not just economics and power.

After reading this book, some readers might conclude that it is about marketing; and they are not entirely wrong. Many imaginative creations are products or services in their own right, each to be marketed to target tourism, investor, migrant or trade markets. However, I hope many readers appreciate that this is not the focus of this book. The point is that imaginative community initiatives are coherent parts of a community positioning, making the whole more than the sum of its parts. Also, not all imaginative community initiatives are marketable products or services. Sometimes they are "just" policies, public spaces or infrastructures that require investments to be made in an imaginative way so as to reinforce identity and positioning. Therefore this book is as much about culture as it is about economics.

Some readers might have concluded by now that this book is about place branding or soft power and they are not entirely wrong either. However, the practice in these fields has become one that is focused on design, catchy gimmicks, advertising and propaganda. I hope that most readers, after reading this book, will conclude that this is exactly what imaginative communities are *not* about. Imaginative communities do real things, making real contributions, and generate social engagement, not just power.

8.1 How we de-market

Marketing has become such a dominant force in modern society that one would think that the concept barely requires explanation. It should be hardly a secret that it is driven by understanding and satisfying market demands. Yet, unfortunately, marketing remains misunderstood by many as just being about promotion. Being much more than that, marketing processes are built around knowing one's (potential) customers, researching their needs and wants, and segmenting the market so as to target the right people. Products and services are then designed, promoted and distributed in such a way as to acquire unique positioning in the minds of those target audiences. It is also referred to as "customer focus".

Popular wisdom suggests that even communities need to market themselves, promote the country, sell the city. I wonder if that is very pertinent and whether customer-driven community engagement is appropriate. Communities are not for sale and the economic dimension is only one perspective. Sure, people need to work, earn a living and finance their future and that of their offspring, but they are also concerned about their health, friendships, environment and cultural identity. Reducing communities to marketable products, therefore, seems inappropriate. What is more, the marketing perspective seems to suggest that the focus needs to be on how we serve market demands. Even if residents are seen as an internal market, is that an appropriate prioritisation of policy agendas? Are non-commercial priorities of wellbeing, sustainability or social inclusion not just as important if not more so? There are modern interpretations of marketing that include an appreciation of these collective demands and maybe my issue is more with commoditisation than with community marketing per se; yet, the practice of it seems to be rather old-fashioned.

Also, of course, one of the essential ways in which communities prosper is to engage in economic exchange with the outside world. Trading and export of commodities, products and services is the most obvious way in which communities earn an income, and it has been an essential part of the economic development of communities for millennia. More recently, the importance of attracting tourists, international students and migrant workers has risen up the policy agenda. In addition, of course, creating investment opportunities and facilitating desirable factor conditions aims to attract foreign direct investment.

All these economic domains, however, have their specialised and legitimate professional organisations: tourism management organisations, investment promotion agencies, export marketing associations and talent attraction agencies. It is perfectly logical that communities set up agencies that segment tourism, investment and export markets in order to position and promote community offerings effectively and efficiently among the right audience. Using promotional tools such as advertising, special offers, direct marketing or public relations under these circumstances is fine, as one is presumably communicating with an audience that is interested in the offer and welcomes the attention (assuming skilful market research, targeting and positioning).

That, obviously, is something completely different from promoting the country or selling the city. Tourism and export marketing, investment promotion and talent attraction are about marketing a product to a target audience, *not* about community boosterism. The confusion is probably caused by the fact that selling a tourism product, an export product or an investment opportunity is much easier for communities that have a strong reputation. Communities that are unknown or unpopular internationally will find it much harder and more expensive to market their offerings. This has been proven over and over again in studies on destination image (tourism marketing research), country-of-origin effects (export marketing research) or location attractiveness (investment decision research).

So marketing requires reputation, which does not mean that the reverse is also true. Boosterish advertising, community propaganda or public relations are not effective or efficient ways to increase exports and bring in more tourists, investments and international students, because it abandons the customer focus logic of marketing products to target markets. Mass communication to broadcast community accomplishments to a global audience, as can be witnessed frequently on CNN or BBC World News, is like shooting with hail to kill a fly. Without intricate targeting, the likelihood of reaching someone in the audience who is actually interested in absorbing what is being communicated is small indeed. Most media consumers will switch off or fail to comprehend why they are being "spoken to". Sure, beautiful cinematography might attract attention, but will it change people's minds?

So while marketing can be effectively and efficiently applied to facilitate economic exchange of community offerings, it seems unsuitable when applied to communities as a whole. This is exactly where imaginative initiatives come in. These are projects and occasionally marketable products in their own right, yet they raise profile and reputation for the community. The Just Peace Festival in The Hague, Austin's South by Southwest (SXSW) Festival, Gaudí's creations as attractions in Barcelona or the resorts on Dubai's Palm Island are all commercial offerings as such. Yet, they have resulted in a raised profile and reputation for the communities involved, because they are compelling and uniquely local.

At the same time, other examples of imaginative initiatives are useful and meaningful in other ways – non-commercial, but still beneficial to the communities. Bhutan's focus on gross national happiness, Oslo's *Future Library*, or the Van Gogh-inspired "starry night" cycle path in the city of Eindhoven are all genuine projects or constructive policies that have a largely non-economic local impact, while at the same time striking a chord with international audiences. In fact, if done well, imaginative initiatives do not require much marketing at all as they will promote themselves in today's social media landscape. While advertising pushes messages onto an unwilling audience, search and social media engagement provide opportunities for a willing audience to pull, enhance and share community experiences and stories that are of interest to self-selected audiences. These are exactly the kind of processes that imaginative communities exploit.

8.2 How we re-brand

So, the attentive reader might wonder, considering that this book is partly about marketable "products" that contribute to reputation, is it about branding? Assuming that indeed, branding is defined as the concerted effort to make something (products, services, corporations, communities, persons, and so on) *identifiably distinctive*, in that case, yes, branding is the long-term strategic approach to building imaginative communities. Consistency in linking community identity with captivating initiatives will build brand equity for the community, as they become more recognisable and associated with positive perceptions.

The problem with the practice of applying branding concepts to communities, cities, regions and countries is that branding is often misinterpreted and the focus is put far too much on superficial aesthetics. In simple terms, branding is about two things: making something identifiable and making it distinctive. The first deals with naming and visual design, the second with meaning (brand positioning, personality, promise, etc.). The most important decision in commercial branding is, of course, naming, which is linked to trademarking. For communities, these kinds of decisions are almost completely irrelevant, as communities have (often long-established) names and those names are usually very hard to protect with a trademark. Yet many communities are still obsessed with consistency in presentation: type fonts, logos, use of colours or slogans. The question is whether that really matters.

Consistent presentation in commercial branding facilitates recognisability in advertising and retail environments; i.e. at the few touchpoints at which consumers engage with a brand. However, obviously, the retail environment is not where communities engage with audiences. Communities are abundantly represented in mainstream news, social media and popular culture. Do logos and slogans, apart from the name, ever get noticed in these environments? There are so many more touchpoints and channels that communities deal with compared to corporations, that it is hard to imagine that consistency in presentation has a real significant impact.

There are reasons why communities rightly spend resources on visual identity. Websites, stationery and business cards need to be designed and clever consistent representation does not hurt. This kind of design expertise, easily purchased, provides officials with prestige and pleasure, not to mention the peer pressure and one-upmanship that is experienced at international exhibitions, conferences, trade fairs and missions. However, what often seems to be forgotten is that trademarks (including logos) only become brands when they represent meaning to external audiences. So, if community branding is reduced to design, then no, this book is not about that at all. What successful imaginative communities do is to aim for long-term presence, positioning and purpose. To achieve that, visual identity is much, much less important than it is in commercial branding.

Yet, governments often wonder how they can enforce the use of their "brand" (they will say "brand' when they mean "logo") and regulate who can and who cannot carry it and in what way. It is the wrong question to ask and asking it is recognition of defeat. A good brand strategy not only builds engagement with the outside world, but also among stakeholders and internal audiences. It should be built on a sense of belonging and shared purpose and hence generate the kind of engagement that is desired and impossible to imitate elsewhere, motivating the internal stakeholders to contribute. This is how 'I ❤NY' and 'I AMsterdam' became successful, not because they are clever design gimmicks (which they are), but because they represent something that people were already proud of or engaged with. Governments in New York City and Amsterdam did not need to strategise about what these logos were to represent and how to build awareness; the equity was already there in the minds of most people, both local stakeholders and global audiences. The logos just helped to create something to characterise that equity (i.e. a brand). Unfortunately, most communities do not have this luxury of a historically built global awareness and reputation and that is exactly why they want to "do something with branding", thinking that 'I ❤...' will help them. It won't (many communities have specifically tried 'I ❤...' and failed). It is not the symbol that builds the reputation, but the symbol can become an icon for an existing reputation that has been painstakingly built over a period of time.

Another part of today's "misunderstanding of branding" is that everything is evaluated in economic terms, so even reputation is seen to be only of interest in as much as it facilitates marketing. At one time reputation was a legitimate goal in its own right, but this is no longer so much the case. Part of the reason is the loss of our religion, but globalisation may also be a factor, as most economic and political activities have become detached from local communities. Investors used to depend on their good name in their community for future business and/or a place in heaven. In today's world, where money is mobile, investors operate across borders and religion has lost its grip on society, reputation has become a means to an end, not an ethical question, but an economic one.

Unfortunately, a marketing approach to community branding (destination branding, investment branding, "made-in" branding) also does not work because of the way people build mental images. Reputations are indivisible networks of associations that people deploy whenever they engage with "the other". Usually, there is no single economic offering (a single tourist attraction, a specific export product or a unique investment offering) dominating the image, and where there is, it has proven to be unhealthy (resulting in over-tourism or economic vulnerabilities). Likewise, representation should also not be limited to specific economic sectors. It runs the risk of being too much demand driven as opposed to being about "who we are, where we came from and what we represent". Imaginative communities need to facilitate cooperation internally and externally, not focus on competition. The latter is the rhetoric of marketing and, unfortunately, more so than it should be, also that of branding.

The focus on competition and the market is counter-productive in community reputation management and hence this book advocates the idea of the imaginative community. Branding is its strategic perspective in building long-term presence, positioning and purpose. The brand concept is by no means obsolete when applied appropriately. It is about appreciating that the reputations and images of communities should - and understanding how they can - incorporate the sense of community and to formulate shared purpose and ideals based on the shared identity, formulating an aspirational strategic vision. Subsequently, it is about operationalising such a vision into a strategy that formulates policies, partnerships and actions that will enable the community to project an unbroken stream of imaginative community initiatives that will deliver the reputation it deserves.

8.3 What we are accountable for

Today, all that we do seems to be made accountable only in financial terms. Successful international community engagement is measured in export value, tourist spending, foreign direct investment influx, number of relocations and international students, ignoring the gap between building public opinion (awareness and reputation) and calls to action (i.e. branding versus marketing). Imaginative communities focus on both hard and soft power, the power of coercion (economic) and the power of appeal (reputation).

In the tourism, investment, diplomacy or export promotion literature there is sufficient evidence to suggest that reputation will influence travel, investment or purchase decisions. In export marketing, the impact of country image on exports is referred to as country-of-origin effect.[27] In international government relations, image effects are considered in cultural or public diplomacy.[28] Investors and international students choose locations partly based on image and reputation.[29] In parallel, tourism research incorporates a considerable body of knowledge explaining how travellers' decision making is influenced by what is referred to as destination image effects;[30] others even argue that there is a close link between community reputation and sports.[31]

All this is summarised in a relevant study by Fetscherin,[32] in which the Anholt-GfK Roper Nation Brands Index™ (NBI™) is compared to the Country Brand Strength Index (CBSI), a composite index that includes actual statistics on visitor arrivals, exports, foreign investment, immigration and governance environment, standardised on a per-capita basis. Figure 9 shows a clear correlation (r=.621, p<.01), indicating that image drives performance and vice versa. However, as one would expect, this is not a one-on-one relationship, as is illustrated by outliers such as Japan, Italy or Brazil, where perception is stronger than reality, or Ireland, the Netherlands, Austria, Switzerland or Belgium, where perception is weaker than reality. So, awareness, image and reputation are the foundations on which to build a strong economy and vice versa, but in addition, many other factors will determine success in export, tourism and investment economics. The former is the domain of branded imaginative communities, the latter that of marketing.

Hence, imaginative community initiatives should be judged on their internal project economics (if any) and their impact on media and public opinion, internally and externally. It would be unfair to judge them primarily on the indirect long-term economic effects on investment, trade, tourism or migration, which are influenced by many other factors (e.g. exchange rates or trade tariffs, to name two significant examples). All those factors being equal, the indirect effect of imaginative community initiatives on overall economic performance (apart from internal project finances) has to be taken for granted, as reputation assists economic performance in the long run (see Figure 9).

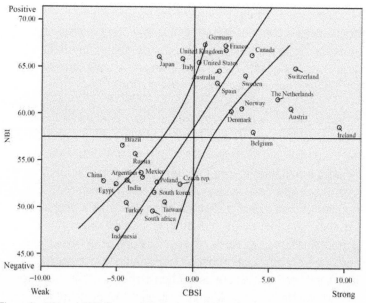

Figure 9: NBI and CBSI (Source: Fetscherin, M. (2010) 'The determinants and measurement of a country brand: the country brand strength index', *International Marketing Review*, 27 (4): 466–79).

As an example, it might be useful to look at events, which are an easy vehicle for imaginative initiatives as we have seen in The Hague, Den Bosch and Austin.

Of course, such events have a budget, require investments and return on those investments (and do their own marketing). The increase in visitor spending and foreign direct investment does not usually outweigh the government spending. Therefore, events are also often made accountable for their long-term economic impact, in terms of legacy effects of infrastructure investments and enhanced attractiveness. Isolating such impacts, however, is virtually impossible, particularly when taking into account the opportunity costs (i.e. would it not have been better to spend government money elsewhere to reach long-term development impacts?).

So the question is: why else would communities host events (or invest in other imaginative initiatives) if not for economic gain or local development? The reason is, of course, the (social) media spotlight. This, if utilised well, potentially raises international awareness and impacts the community's reputation externally and civic pride internally. In Chapter 7 we looked at the case of Germany hosting the FIFA World Cup in 2006. They benefited – and possibly still do – from a nudged reputation in which Germans are seen as friendlier, more fun and welcoming than they were before. It has also raised international self-confidence among Germans themselves. So, if anything, even if the event was an economic burden, at least Germany was able to use the media spotlight to its long-term advantage. That is what imaginative community initiatives, besides their direct internal economics, should be accountable for.

External media image (Chapter 6), reputation (Chapter 5) and stakeholder engagement/community pride (Chapter 2) should be the main measures of accountability for imaginative initiatives and mega-events. So it is shocking to see that more often than not, mega-events and other white elephants are presented as just another publicity stunt, a project of political prestige, often even ignoring the impact on local populations and their retaliation. This clearly has to change.

This logic can also be turned around, whenever communities are dealing with negative perceptions. The standard reaction is to tweak the economics: lower taxes, improve productivity, attract investment, lower the export barriers or subsidise tourism. Rarely is the question asked, whether the perception issue is really the result of economic reality. Is it maybe a deeper-rooted effect of local identity/geography/mentality of the community (such as the Germans were able to admit in terms of their welcoming nature prior to the FIFA World Cup 2006)? Is it maybe the result of widespread persistent clichés and stereotypes (for instance the common assumption that Germans are formal and have no sense of humour)? Could it be that it involves media framing? Journalists are eager to appease their audience by confirming their preconceived ideas (an event in Germany, for instance, cannot be a success as Germans are unfriendly). Or lastly, is it maybe a self-fulfilling prophecy because of our own reactions? Very often, spokespersons, politicians and stakeholder representatives become upset and offended when clichés and stereotypes are reconfirmed by publics and the media as a consequence of news events or otherwise. Persisting in such defensive reactions might actually result in associations becoming even more tenacious. What imaginative communities do is to change the narrative, by uplifting the community, influencing the media agenda and gradually seeping through into the consciousness of outsiders.

Endnotes

[1] Land Department (2010). *Annual Transactions. Government of Dubai.* Retrieved on 4 January 2010 from http://www.dubailand.gov.ae/ld_website/English/transactions/Yearly_Transactions.aspx.

[2] UNESCO Institute for Statistics (UIS). http://data.uis.unesco.org/, Retrieved on 30 March 2017.

[3] WORLD VALUES SURVEY Wave 6 2010–2014 OFFICIAL AGGREGATE v.20140429. World Values Survey Association (www.worldvaluessurvey.org). Aggregate File Producer: Asep/JDS, Madrid SPAIN.

[4] Verheul, W.J. (2015). 'Plaatsgebonden identiteit. Het anker voor stedelijke ontwikkeling'. In: Hafkamp, W., J. Koffijberg, T. Rutjens, G. Teisman (eds), *De stad kennen, de stad maken.* Den Haag: Platform31.

[5] Halman, L. (2001). *The European Values Study 1999.* Tilburg: WORC.

[6] Govers, R. & Go, F.M. (2009). *Place Branding: Glocal, virtual and physical, identities constructed, imagined and experienced.* Basingstoke, Hampshire (UK): Palgrave Macmillan.

[7] Flycatcher (2010). *Kwartaalonderzoek imago van provincie: Uitsplitsing Limburgers op speciale vraag van provincie,* http://www.flycatcher.eu/nld/panel/nieuws/?newsid=252.

[8] *Kroniek der stad Roermond.* In Venner, J. (2009) *Canon van Limburg,* bvLimburg & Mooi Limburgs Boekenfonds.

[9] ESPON (2007) *ESPON project 1.4.3: Study on Urban Functions,* European Union http://www.espon.eu/export/sites/default/Documents/Projects/ESP

ON2006Projects/StudiesScientificSupportProjects/UrbanFunctions/fr-1.4.3_April2007-final.pdf

[10] Palfreyman, D. & Al Khalil, M. (2003). '"A Funky Language for Teenzz to Use": representing Gulf Arabic in Instant Messaging'. *Journal of Computer Mediated Communication* 9 (1): [Online], Retrieved on 30 December 2008 from http://jcmc.indiana.edu/vol9/issue1/palfreyman.html).

[11] Heller, N. (2017). 'Estonia, the digital republic', *The New Yorker*, 18 & 25 December.

[12] Schulte Nordholt, J.W (1985). *Triomf en tragiek van de vrijheid: De geschiedenis van de verenigde Staten van America*. Amsterdam: Informatief.

[13] Lehner, M. (1997). *The Complete Pyramids*. London: Thames and Hudson, p.9.

[14] Maggi, S. (1983). *Roma, I Fori*. Novara: Istituto Geografico De Agostini SpA.

[15] Ministry for Foreign Affairs of Finland (2017). Presentation at the City Nation Place Conference in London, 8 November.

[16] De Beer, I. & Van Buitenen, A. (2016). 'Leveraging stakeholder interests in public diplomacy: The case of the Hague Peace and Justice Project', *Place branding and Public Diplomacy*, 12 (4), pp. 329–338.

[17] European Commission (2014). 'Erasmus Impact Study confirms EU student exchange scheme boosts employability and job mobility'. Accessed on 8 August 2017 via http://europa.eu/rapid/press-release_IP-14-1025_en.htm

[18] Riedl, John & Joseph Konstan (2002). *Word of Mouse: The Marketing Power of Collaborative Filtering*. New York: Warner Books.

[19] Alcantara, N. (2004). 'Movies and television shows help boost tourism'. *eTurboNews*. 14 July, Retrieved from http://www.travelwirenews.com

[20] Keen, A. (2007). *The Cult of the Amateur: How Today's Internet Is Killing Our Culture and Assaulting Our Economy*. London: Nicholas Brealey.

[21] Schatz, R. & Kolmer, C. (2010). 'News Coverage of Foreign Place Brands: Implication for Communication'. In: F.M. Go and R. Govers (eds), *International Place Branding Yearbook 2010: Place branding in the new age of innovation* (pp. 134–46). Basingstoke, Hampshire: Palgrave Macmillan.

[22] Cromwell, T. (2011). 'The East West Nation Brand Perception Indexes and Reports: Perception Measurement and Nation Branding'. In: F.M. Go and R. Govers (eds), *International Place Branding Yearbook 2011: Managing Reputational Risk* (pp. 102–11). Basingstoke, Hampshire: Palgrave Macmillan.

[23] Paul, D.E. (2004). 'World Cities as Hegemonic Projects: The politics of global imagineering in Montreal', *Political Geography*, 23 (5), p. 573.

[24] Yeoh, B. (2005). 'The global cultural city? Spatial imagineering and politics in the (multi) cultural marketplaces of South-east Asia', *Urban Studies*, 42 (5), p. 947.

[25] The Imagineers (1998). *Walt Disney Imagineering: A Behind the Dreams Look at Making the Magic Real by the Imagineers*. New York: Hyperion, cover page.

[26] Tolosa, L. (2001). *Barcelona, Gaudí y la Ruta del Modernismo*. Madrid: Kliczkowski Publishers.

[27] See, for instance,Verlegh, P.W.J. (2010) 'Country Images: Why They Influence Consumers', in: F.M. Go and R. Govers (eds), *International Place Branding Yearbook: Place branding in the new age of innovation, Vol 1* (pp. 45–54). Basingstoke, Hampshire: Palgrave Macmillan.

[28] See, for instance, Van Ham, P. (2008) 'Place Branding: The State of the Art', *The Annals of the American Academy of Political and Social Science*, 616 (1), pp. 126–49.

[29] See, for instance, Cubillo, J.M., Sánchez, J., & Cerviño, J. (2006) 'International students' decision-making process', *International Journal of Educational Management*, 20 (2), pp. 101–15; Hodgkinson, A. & Nyland, C. (2001) 'Space, subjectivity and the investment location decision', *The Journal of Industrial Relations*, 43 (4), pp. 438–61.

[30] See, for instance, Echtner, C.M. & Ritchie, J.R.B. (2003) 'The Meaning and Measurement of Destination Image', *Journal of Tourism Studies*, 14 (1), pp. 37–48;

Tapachai, N. & Waryszak, R. (2000) 'An Examination of the Role of Beneficial Image in Tourist Destination Selection', *Journal of Travel Research*, 39 (1) August, pp. 37–44.

[31] Rein, I. & Shields, B. (2007). 'Place branding sports: Strategies for differentiating emerging, transitional, negatively viewed and newly industrialised nations', *Place Branding and Public Diplomacy*, 3 (1), pp. 73–85.

[32] Fetscherin, M. (2010). 'The determinants and measurement of a country brand: the country brand strength index', *International Marketing Review*, 27 (4), pp. 466–79.

Index

About the author

Since 2009 Robert Govers has co-edited and authored four books on the topic of community reputation with Palgrave Macmillan publishers. *Imaginative Communities* is his first book published under his own imprint. He has also co-authored over 50 journal articles, book chapters and conference papers and has delivered numerous public speeches and business publications. In addition, he is co-editor of the quarterly journal, *Place Branding and Public Diplomacy*.

Robert Govers is an independent international adviser, scholar, speaker and author on the reputation of cities, regions and countries. He is chairman of the International Place Branding Association and the managing research partner of www.good.country. He has also been an adjunct or visiting scholar at Tsinghua University, Beijing; the Indian School of Business, Hyderabad; the University of Leuven, Belgium; Rotterdam School of Management, the Netherlands; Loughborough University London Campus; IULM University Milano, Italy; and several institutes in Dubai, United Arab Emirates. He also teaches place branding on the UNESCO World Heritage at Work Master's programme in Torino, Italy.

Robert typically advises in areas such as place identity, image, reputation, economic competitiveness, tourism policy and strategy, educational policy, tourism and investment promotion, and major international events. This is approached from a strategic reputation management perspective referred to as competitive identity, which is based on the premise that places build reputation through substance and symbolic actions, as opposed to marketing gimmicks.

Robert has held positions in South Africa, the Netherlands, Belgium and Dubai, United Arab Emirates. He has been involved in many consultancy projects and advisory boards for reputable organisations such as the International Air Transport Association, the European Commission, the Flemish government and various ministries, tourism promotion boards, and regional and city administrations.

Robert has both a doctoral (2005) and master's degree (1995) from the Rotterdam School of Management, Erasmus University, the Netherlands.

www.rgovers.com
www.twitter.com/rgovers
www.linkedin.com/in/rgovers

Lightning Source UK Ltd.
Milton Keynes UK
UKHW010630010920
369159UK00001B/270